Masters of Music

Masters of Music

Their Works, Their Lives, Their Times

Dorothy and Joseph Samachson

Doubleday & Company, Inc., Garden City, New York

CONTENTS

LIST OF ILLUSTRATIONS

Masters of Music

PREFACE

"Music begins where words fail," said the poet Heine, expressing in words that do not fail some of the meaning and the importance of music. But if words fail, the reader may ask, why have we written so many of them about music and musicians?

They are certainly no substitute for music itself. They can, however, help us to enjoy and appreciate it. For, although music has been called an international language, it is nothing of the sort. Music is many languages, and sometimes the listeners who understand one misunderstand the others. Most of the music of Haydn, Mozart, and Beethoven was appreciated at first hearing. Other composers have not been so fortunate. Major compositions of Mussorgsky, Debussy, and Stravinsky have been accepted only gradually and grudgingly.

In one way or another, the life of a composer finds expression in his music. His hopes and fears, joys and sorrows, loves and hates are transformed into sounds, sometimes quite unexpected ones. We hope that this book, by contributing to a knowledge of the lives of different composers, will help the reader the better to understand why they wrote as they did, and to enjoy listening to music that at first hearing may seem rather strange.

We have tried to keep our personal likes and dislikes to a minimum, but we cannot keep them out entirely. They are reflected, to some extent, even by our choice of composers to write about. We believe that the choice has been a reasonably fair one, and we hope that the reader will feel the same way about it.

I

MAN AND MUSIC
IN THE VERY BEGINNING

The first human music, so far as we can tell, was created and performed, not for the pleasure of the listener, but because of its magical powers. Primitive tribes clapped their hands together or pounded on tree trunks to create rhythms, while medicine men chanted, sang, or danced—all for the purpose of ensuring success in a hunt, chasing away evil spirits, or making rain.

For tens of thousands of years, the human race struggled merely to survive in a world filled with hostile forces. In this struggle, Man acquired many new skills. He learned how to till the soil, to domesticate cows and sheep, to weave cloth, and to work with clay and metals. Many of these skills he considered so remarkable that he would not even take credit for developing them. He regarded them as gifts of the gods, and he composed songs and dances to thank the gods for their generosity.

When he developed written languages, and established the first villages, towns, and nations—when, to put it briefly, he became civilized—his use of music kept pace with his other activities.

One of the first civilized peoples, the Sumerians, lived in the Near East about 3000 B.C. They developed mathematics and astronomy and put these sciences to use for such purposes as telling time (we still use the system of minutes and seconds they devised) and irrigating the soil. Ur, home town of the patriarch

1. *A Sumerian lyre, reconstructed by archaeologists from parts found in the Royal Cemetery at Ur. (Courtesy University Museum, University of Pennsylvania)*

Abraham, was a Sumerian city, and the biblical tale of the Flood is one of the heritages of Sumerian culture.

The Sumerians felt strongly the beauty of music, and their legends even told of animals who responded to it. The music they played and sang was composed by musician priests whose names we do not know. On clay tablets they listed different types of songs—war songs, religious songs, victory songs, even love and work songs. To accompany their singing, they also used musical instruments. In the ruins of the Temple of Ur, archaeologists have found a lyre, and the remains of a harp that belonged to Queen Shubad. This harp, which has been reconstructed, was adorned with gold and precious stones and must have been of great beauty.

The ancient Egyptians also enjoyed music. Wall paintings and sculptures make it clear that the Egyptians played music for pleasure, as well as for religious purposes. Hieroglyphics, the ancient form of Egyptian writing, name several composers who boasted of their talents.

The Old Testament contains many references to the importance of music in the lives of the ancient Hebrews. In Genesis, the first book of the Bible, Jubal is cited as the father of all musical-instrument makers. Music was performed to celebrate victories, and Moses and the children of Israel danced and sang a song to the Lord in thanks for their safe crossing of the Red Sea. Later on, making use of music's magical powers, Joshua sent the

2. *Egyptian musicians. The instruments, from left to right, are a harp, lute, double aulos (reed pipe), and lyre. Wall painting from a Theban tomb, XVIIIth dynasty (1580–1350 B.C.). (Courtesy Metropolitan Museum of Art)*

walls of Jericho tumbling down with the blasts of seven trumpets, and still later, David used music as mental therapy, soothing the troubled mind of King Saul with the peaceful sounds of a harp.

Many musical instruments are mentioned in the Bible. We read of harps and psalteries, of timbrels, of cornets and cymbals. A psaltery is something like a zither, and a timbrel is a kind of tambourine. However, we must remember that the translators of the Bible, more than two thousand years after it was written, had never seen the biblical instruments, and simply gave them names with which they themselves were familiar. All we can be sure of is that the Hebrews knew a number of instruments of different kinds, some stringed, others of metal, some to be struck and others to be used as horns.

We cannot be sure whether the music that David played was of his own creation or whether he was merely performing what someone else had composed. In biblical times, and even much later, it did not seem important to distinguish between the man who created a song and the man who sang it. The chances are that David was improvising, singing what came to him on the spur of the moment. As there was then no way to write down a melody, the music that he played and sang is lost to us forever.

When songs were passed on from one musician to another, it was by ear alone. Folk songs have been kept alive in this manner for centuries, but they are always more or less changed in the process. Music for religious ceremonies changed less than other music, as the priests in the temple were responsible for keeping the services the same from day to day.

The prayers and chants the Hebrews used were probably included in the early Christian rituals. Some scholars claim that the Yemenite Jews, who remained in the Near East, isolated from other musical influences for many centuries, still play and sing the sort of music performed in biblical times. It is unlikely that any music coming down to us would sound exactly as it sounded over two thousand years ago.

Some ancient peoples tried to write down their music, but we do not know what methods they used. At best their systems of

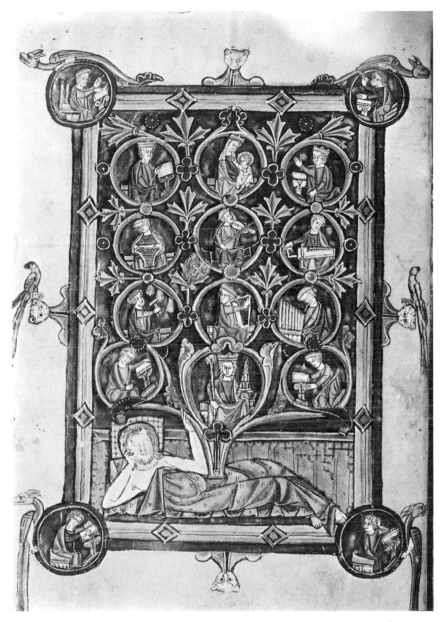

3. Tree of Jesse. A fifteenth-century representation of King David's family
tree. The musical instruments are not authentically biblical, but those familiar
to the artist who drew the tree. (Courtesy Trustees of the British Museum)

notation were clumsy and not very useful, or they would have been adopted by musicians in general, and we would have more information about them.

Between 600 and 500 B.C., the Greeks came upon the musical scene. The Greeks—at first a few groups of aggressive and largely uncivilized conquerors—over many centuries formed a system of city-states in which slaves did almost all the routine work, and the citizens enjoyed a great deal of leisure. Originally, many of the slaves were more civilized than the Greeks themselves, but the Greeks learned from them and, excelling their teachers, raised sculpture, philosophy, science, and literature to a level that we still marvel at.

It was in Greece that the first musicologists and music critics appeared. These were men who wrote *about* music, instead of writing or playing the music itself. The role of music in daily life was glorified. Plato, Aristotle, and other philosophers wrote about the importance of music in education. They felt that the study of music, which included poetry and dance, was more important than gymnastics or physical culture. Music, they thought, purified and enriched the soul, which was more important than the body.

Along with the appreciation of music as art and as a fit subject for philosophy went an increased knowledge of music in relation to science. About 550 B.C., Pythagoras, who has been remembered by generations of students because of the theorem of geometry named after him, studied the relation between the length of a string and the note it produced when set into vibration. He found that, when the string was divided into equal halves, each part, when made to vibrate, produced a note that resembled the original note and yet sounded much higher. Later, musicians counted eight notes from the original note to the upper one, and the musical interval between them became known as the *octave,* or eighth.

As the lyre and other stringed instruments were played long before Pythagoras was born, the octave was almost certainly known before Pythagoras studied it.

Aristoxenus of Tarentum (a Greek colony in Southern Italy) wrote about the theory of music. The Greeks composed in

4. A kithara player and his audience decorate Athenian pottery (450–440 B.C.). (Courtesy Metropolitan Museum of Art, Rogers Fund, 1921)

modes, which were sequences of notes within the range of an octave. Each mode had its own sequence of notes and its own name and character. Composers were taught that the Mixolydian mode was best for sad music, the Phrygian for relaxed music, the Dorian for martial music, and so on. The modes became the basis of the major and minor scales familiar to musicians today.

The Greeks used two systems of notation, one for voice, the other for instruments. Only a few fragments of these systems have been discovered, and we still do not know how to interpret their notation, or how the ancient Greek music sounded.

The Greek democracies gave their citizens a great deal of free time in which to enjoy the arts and other forms of entertainment. They liked to attend contests of all kinds—not only in athletics, but in poetry and drama as well. The poets chanted or sang their poems, while the dramatists wrote verses that were also set to music. In addition, the Greeks held purely instrumental contests. We know, for instance, of a lyre-playing contest that took place about 550 B.C.

With all their philosophy and theory, the Greeks still retained some of the primitive belief that music had magical powers.

In Greek mythology, the Muses, nine beautiful goddesses, ruled the arts. Six of them represent music, poetry, and dance. But they were not the only divine patrons of music. The god Hermes was said to have invented the lyre, which he presented to Apollo, his fellow-god, as a gift. Pan, the satyr, played the syrinx, a group of small reed whistles tied together, which to this day is called Pan's pipe. The mythical hero Orpheus played the lyre so beautifully that he moved gods, mortals, and even animals to tears, and Aesculapius, the half god whom the Greeks regarded as the father of medicine, used music in the treatment of his patients. On the other hand, music was also used for evil purposes. Homer, in the *Odyssey*, tells of the Sirens, dreadful sea creatures whose songs were so irresistibly beautiful that they lured sailors to their deaths.

The Greeks also had a number of myths about vain and foolhardy mortals who dared to pit themselves against the gods in musical contests. One man, Maryas, found a flute of Athena's and challenged Apollo to a contest. Naturally, he lost and, as was customary in myths, he paid for his defeat with his life. Another mortal, who boasted of his talents on the trumpet, was drowned by the sea-god, Triton, the original trumpeter.

During the period we call the Golden Age of Greece, about 500–400 B.C., the character of both musicians and their music changed. Musicians became more professional and, like the professional poets and sculptors, achieved recognition for the talents with which they enriched everyday life. Music became less important in religious rites, which were carried out mainly by the priests, and more important in the entertainment world.

The Romans, who followed the Greeks on the stage of the Western world's history, had little musical heritage of their own. By the time they conquered the Greeks, however, they had taken over much of the art and science known to what they considered the civilized world. The Romans too used music to worship their gods, but musicians also put their talents at the service of rich patrons, and many of them became wealthy. They were in great demand at parties, and the presence of a noted musician was sometimes all that was needed to make a banquet a social success.

Ancient Rome, like modern Hollywood, thrived on lavish spectacles, and music accompanied performances in the Roman arena. Many of the compositions might properly have been called "Music to Kill and Die by," for among the favorite Roman pastimes were battles to the death between gladiators, between men and beasts, or between such wild animals as tigers and elephants. The degrading nature of these spectacles helped brutalize both the musicians who composed for them and the spectators who watched and listened.

Music education was less important in Rome than in Greece, and the Romans contributed little of their own to music. They did develop and improve several instruments, and they are credited with introducing the bagpipe to the natives when they invaded the British Isles.

Although the professionals were better musicians, the playing of a few imperial Roman amateurs has received more attention from historians of music. The musician whose name is most familiar to us is the Emperor Nero (A.D. 37–68). Whenever he played, probably the lyre or the water organ, audiences were forced to listen and critics to praise him on pain of death. Historians refer frequently to his playing and singing, especially to the performance he is said to have given during the burning of

5. *A Roman lady playing the kithara. From a fresco, first century* B.C. (*Courtesy Metropolitan Museum of Art, Rogers Fund, 1903*)

Rome in A.D. 64. He has also been accused of ordering the murder of Brittanicus, another Roman, not so much because Brittanicus was a rival for the throne as because Nero envied his musical ability.

With the rise of Christianity and the fall of the Roman Empire in A.D. 476, the musicians who performed for pleasure and entertainment faced a bleak future. The early Christian church, revolted by the excesses of the pagan world and by its use of the arts for worldly pleasure, tried to banish music from daily life and reserve it for religious ceremonies.

The enjoyment of music as a form of art seemed to come to an end, so that during the next thousand years music appeared to have no history. Nowadays, historians know that the attempt to banish music from daily life did not, in fact, succeed. The Church could not stop a housewife from singing a lullaby to her infant, or a child from beating out rhythms on a wooden rail, or a shepherd from making a simple wind instrument from a reed.

These rhythms and melodies of the common people were not written down. Yet it was during this long dark period of ignorance, pestilence, and almost unceasing war that music as we know it was slowly coming into being all over Europe.

II

COMPOSER AND MUSICIAN IN
THE MIDDLE AGES

In their reaction to the use of music for vulgar or brutal forms of entertainment, the early Christians ascribed an evil nature to musical instruments. St. Jerome, for instance, warned that no young girl should be exposed to the sight of a musical instrument lest she be corrupted. The singing of melodious and strongly rhythmic songs was also forbidden. The one musical activity that was not only permitted but encouraged was the chanting by the congregation attending services of a single melody with a weak or uncertain rhythm.

The early days of Christianity saw violent conflict among different creeds. In order to keep the Church united, all religious groups were required to conduct their services in the same way. St. Ambrose (c. 340–97), Bishop of Milan, organized and introduced a unified liturgy, or church ritual, which included the chanting of specific hymns and psalms. Some of these chants are still in use.

Nevertheless, with religious services going on in such widely separated places as France and North Africa—and in those days communication was difficult and dangerous—local differences in the use of music did spring up. In the sixth century, Pope Gregory I (c. 540–604) ordered the different chants compiled and assigned to specific services. These chants, or plain songs, simple unaccompanied melodies, were used by the Catholic Church for centuries and are still known as Gregorian chants.

Pope Gregory hoped that this reform would establish the proper religious music once and for all. But without a reliable form of notation, this hope was vain. How was a bishop sent by the pope to tell whether the same notes were being sung by a congregation in France as by one he had heard three months before in Spain or Italy? Unless he had a very good ear and a perfect memory, he would unknowingly permit all sorts of changes to be made. And there would be more changes the year after, and the year after that.

Many attempts were made to develop a useful form of notation. One such attempt was made by the Roman scholar Boethius (c. 470–c. 525), who devised a system in which tones were represented by letters of the alphabet. In the seventh century, however, musicians started on the track that eventually led to our present system. They began to use *neumes,* signs that could vary in shape from little squares to exclamation points. When these neumes were placed above the words of a chant, they indicated the rise and fall of the melody, as well as the approximate length of time each note should be held and the degree of emphasis it needed. In some manuscripts, a single staff line was also present. During the next four centuries, the use of neumes increased, but so did dissatisfaction with their weaknesses. For one thing, the person who read the neumes had no way of telling how high the melody should rise or how low it should fall.

In the eleventh century, Guido of Arezzo (c. 995–c. 1050), a Benedictine monk who was also a musician, placed his neumes above or below the lines of a four-line staff. It is not certain that Guido himself was the first to have this idea, but he is usually given credit for it. At any rate, his notation led eventually to the notation of the present, in which five-line staves are used and egg-shaped notes represent different tones by their positions on or off the lines. But even the crude system used in Guido's time made it possible for composers to write down their melodies with much greater accuracy than before.

By this time, composers were writing not only for human voices but for many instruments as well. The organ, primitive forms of

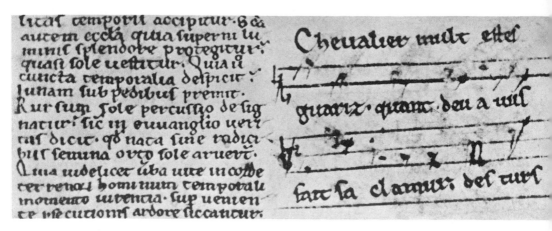

6. The oldest French song in manuscript utilizing neumes on lines. From about 1144. (New York Public Library)

which had existed in biblical times, was introduced into churches, lending its powerful voice in support of the chorus, and in some cases drowning the human voices. For nonreligious music, the *vielle*, ancestor of the modern violin, was very popular. Musicians also played the harp, psaltery (from which the harpsichord descended), the lute, trumpet, shawm (a small reed instrument), and small portable organs. Some of these instruments were first known in ancient Greece and Rome, others were imported from

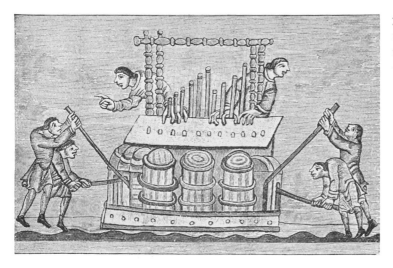

7. An organ of the twelfth century. Note the four men needed to work the bellows. (New York Public Library)

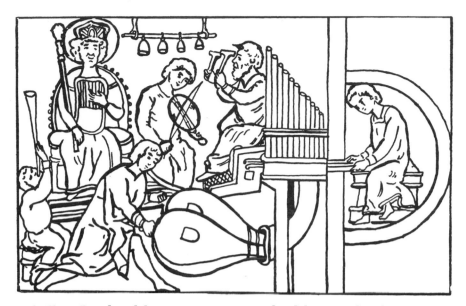

8. *King David and his musicians, as visualized by a medieval artist. The instruments are a horn, lyre, vielle, bells, and organ. (New York Public Library)*

the East, and still others were invented and improved in Europe. Paintings made in the Middle Ages show us what they looked like and how they changed from one century to the next.

While these changes were going on, the common people continued to sing the folk songs and dance the folk dances that had been passed on from generation to generation. Folk melodies also appeared, with new words set to them, in the miracle and morality plays, where actors sang and danced to break the monotony of serious dialogue. Although the more imaginative performers composed many new songs for their own use, the lazier or less imaginative ones preferred to adapt the old tunes.

New types of professional musicians appeared. Itinerant entertainers called *jongleurs,* or jugglers, not only performed acrobatic tricks but sang, played, and danced in market places and village squares. These jongleurs had a bad reputation, which they often deserved, as many of them were also pickpockets, thieves, and confidence men. But they were also the people who spread music from one village to another, showed their listeners what the new musical instruments could do, and added a rare pleasure to the dull lives of medieval peasants and townspeople.

Some of the jongleurs acquired permanent jobs with the nobility and were called minstrels. They were hired to compose and play music for the dancing and singing of their employers. Their lives were usually considered so carefree, gay, and profitable that many youngsters ran off to join their ranks.

Between the eleventh and fourteenth centuries, the European countries, including England, engaged in a series of holy wars known as Crusades. They were intended to rescue Jerusalem from the Saracens, but despite the loss of hundreds of thousands of lives, they failed. For those who survived, however, the Crusades were highly educational. Among other things, the Christian armies learned each other's songs and dances and had an opportunity to hear Eastern music, as well as to acquire musical instruments in the countries they looted.

With the Age of Chivalry, which began during the Crusades, a new group of composing and performing musicians arose. They were the troubadours, or *trouvères,* as they were called in France. Most of them were knights and noblemen. Very conscious of their dignity as artists, they composed romantic ballads to

9. *Minstrels of the fifteenth century. From a sculpture in St. Mary's Church in Beverly, England. (New York Public Library)*

10. *Troubadours playing their instruments.* (*New York Public Library*)

celebrate the virtues of their ladyloves or the heroic feats of kings. The troubadours did not hesitate to steal from their social inferiors, and it is possible that they often received credit for songs that were really the creation of the jongleurs and minstrels.

At any rate, with songs of their own creation or not, they were active in France, Spain, Italy, and England. In Germany, they were called minnesingers.

Richard the Lion-Hearted (1157–99), King of England and a leader in one of the Crusades, was a troubadour whose rescue from an Austrian prison is a well-known English tale. His minstrel, Blondel, is said to have risked his life wandering through Austria in search of the king. Outside the walls of one fortress after another, he sang a ballad composed by Richard himself, until he heard the answering verse sung by Richard in his dungeon. Then returned to England and arranged for the payment of ransom to free Richard.

One of the most outstanding professional troubadours was Adam de la Halle (c. 1235–c. 87). For some reason, he was called "The Hunchback of Arras," although he himself denied that he had this physical handicap. He worked in France and Italy and he wrote many songs as well as musical dramas.

With so much new music being played and sung, the more talented and adventurous church musicians were not satisfied to keep writing simple melodies like those of the Gregorian chants. They began to adorn their melodies with extra notes, and to introduce nonreligious tunes and harmonies. In some cases church authorities were horrified to discover that their organists or choir directors had palmed off as religious music melodies that were

11. Itinerant musicians of the sixteenth century. The "jongleur" tradition has continued in one form or another to present times. (New York Public Library)

originally sung with antireligious words, some even glorifying drunkenness or lewdness.

Some musicians went so far that Pope John XXII (c. 1244–1334) threatened them with the loss of their jobs unless they stopped writing immoral music for religious services. Other prelates repeated the pope's warnings. But the control of all life by the Church was being challenged by the rise of powerful princes, wealthy merchants, and strong guilds of artisans, and these

12. *A minstrel performing for Queen Mary of France. From a thirteenth-century manuscript.* (*New York Public Library*)

threats could not be enforced. Moreover, music was now so important a part of the services that the musicians knew they were needed, and were not easily frightened. In time, the clergy reconciled itself to the new music, which seemed less and less immoral as time went on. Later, the popes themselves became great patrons of music, and toward the end of the fifteenth century, music was given its own patron saint, St. Cecilia.

Despite the continuing difficulties of travel, the reputations of fine musicians were becoming more international. In the early fifteenth century, an Englishman, John Dunstable (c. 1370–1453) founded a school of music in the Netherlands, which then included not only Holland but Belgium and Luxembourg as well. Although some of Dunstable's music still survives, we know very little of his life, except that he was reputed to be an astrologer and mathematician. We do know that the musicians he trained soon came to be regarded as the best in Europe, and were invited to the wealthiest courts.

Some time after Dunstable's death, Josquin de Pres (c. 1445–1521) became one of the leaders of the Netherlands school. He worked and performed in such diverse places as the court of Louis

13. *St. Cecilia, patroness of music, holding a portable organ. Engraving by Marcantonio after Raphael. (Courtesy Metropolitan Museum of Art, Dick Fund, 1917)*

XII in Paris, the Papal Chapel, and the court of the Sforza family in Milan. He wrote many motets, Masses, songs, and other compositions. Among his admirers were popes, kings, and princes.

The latter half of the fifteenth century saw the beginning of a giant leap forward in the arts and sciences. This new wave of activity was called the Renaissance, or Rebirth. At about the same time, Johann Gutenberg reinvented printing (the Chinese had invented it hundreds of years before), Constantinople fell to the Turks, and many distinguished scholars fled to Western Europe, bringing their knowledge and skill with them. Soon after, Columbus discovered the New World.

In all this ferment, music too was changing. In the early part of the sixteenth century, Martin Luther (1483–1546) broke away from the Catholic Church in Germany and founded the Lutheran Church. The old religious services were replaced by new ones, and the new ones required new music. Luther, himself a musician, composed both the words and music of hymns that are still sung in Protestant churches. After Luther, music in both Catholic and Protestant churches flourished as never before.

The courts of Europe had become centers of culture and learning. The nobility hired musicians to compose for private church services and for ballets, theatrical spectacles, and entertainments of all kinds.

The human voice was still the most important of all musical instruments, but it was now being used in new ways. In the early songs, every member of a chorus sang the same note (or an octave higher or lower, depending on the range of his voice). Now the more popular forms of music were written for a number of voices singing different melodies at the same time. This sort of music was called polyphonic, or many-voiced, and the writing of melodies so that the notes of one did not clash with those of the others became known as counterpoint.

One kind of song written for many voices, the *madrigal,* was created in Italy. Many madrigals have survived to the present day and have been recorded.

A noted madrigal composer was Don Carlo Gesualdo, Prince of

14. Martin Luther, musician, founder of the Lutheran Church. From the painting by Cranach. (New York Public Library)

Venosa (1560–1613). Some of his songs are considered to be musically far in advance of his time. Gesualdo led a violent personal life, and is also remembered as a murderer. He killed his wife and child and the man he suspected of being his wife's lover.

The two outstanding composers of the sixteenth century, Giovanni Pierluigi da Palestrina (c. 1525–94), and Orlando di Lasso (c. 1530–94), led less violent lives. Palestrina studied music in Rome and spent most of his life there. He held important positions as organist and choir director of St. Peter's Basilica, and was appointed choirmaster of the Sistine Chapel by Pope Julius III. This chapel, used by the popes themselves, is the room on whose ceilings and walls Michelangelo worked for years painting magnificent murals.

Unfortunately, Palestrina did not enjoy the inspiration of these paintings for more than five years. Because he was a married man, he was dismissed by the next Pope, Paul IV, and although he received an appointment in another church, his salary was low, and he had a difficult time earning a living.

Only as he approached the age of fifty did he attain some financial security. In 1571 he was invited back to St. Peter's Basilica and was even given the honorary title of master composer of the Sistine Chapel, although he still was not allowed to work in the chapel itself. He was offered good positions in other cities, but he preferred to live and work in Rome. He continued to compose music for the Church, and even most of the madrigals he wrote were of a religious nature. When he died, he was buried in St. Peter's in a coffin that bore the title "Prince of Music."

Orlando di Lasso, whose name is also written as Lassus or de Lattre, was born in Mons, now part of Belgium. While he was still a child, his voice was considered so beautiful that attempts were made to kidnap him for service in various chapel choirs. This method of acquiring talent was then not uncommon.

Lasso spent many years in Italy and later in Germany, where he was chapelmaster in the Bavarian court. He composed music and rehearsed the choir for the king's private religious services. Lasso was a prolific composer of all types of music and wrote in the

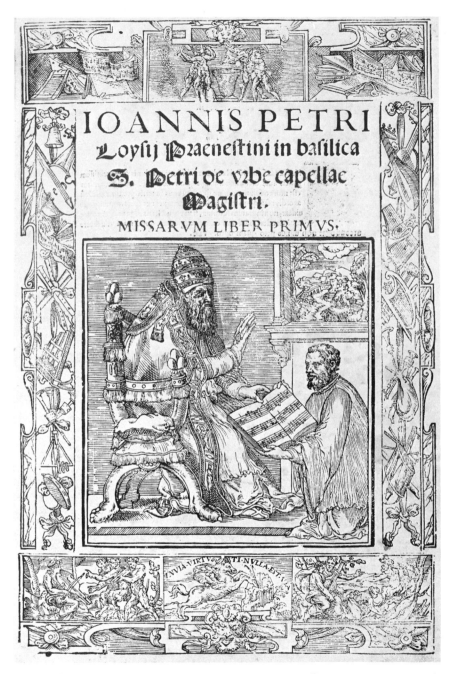

15. *Palestrina presenting the score of a Mass to the pope in St. Peter's Basilica. (Courtesy Library of Congress)*

Italian, French, and German styles then popular. He was elevated to the nobility, was made a papal knight, and was showered with honors and riches.

Lasso was one of the luckier composers. For others, life was neither so full nor so pleasant. It was true that every minor prince or duke who wanted to be in style had his own chapel and chapelmaster, and that this custom made work for some of the composers of that period. But the pay was usually low, and in most courts, the composer was treated merely as a servant.

To add to his worries, he was never sure of the future. He had to go to those churches and courts that wanted him, and whenever an old ruler died or was overthrown in the struggles that continually went on among princes, popes, and kings, he was likely to be out of a job. Meanwhile, whether he himself was poor or rich —and usually it was the former—he enriched the lives of his listeners with the wealth of melody that in those days seemed to flow so easily from every composer's pen.

III

FROM THE RENAISSANCE
TO THE BAROQUE

The Renaissance was a time of tremendous excitement. While politicians and religious leaders fought bitterly for power, the arts and sciences flourished. Astronomers explored the heavens, and daring sailors explored the earth. Merchants sent their ships from one seaport to another, bringing to a newly awakened Europe the silks and spices of the Orient, the corn and potatoes of the New World.

More and more books were being printed, but the printing of musical compositions turned out to be more difficult than the printing of words. The notes and the lines had to be printed separately, and most printers found it impossible to put the notes in exactly the right places on the lines. In 1491 the problem appeared to be solved, and a publisher in Venice produced printed music in which notes and lines fitted well. But the new method was so expensive that, for a long time, almost all music continued to be copied by hand.

Old musical instruments were transformed and new ones were invented. The most popular instrument of the fifteenth century, and for perhaps two centuries after that, was the lute, a plucked string instrument that dates back to antiquity, and was probably introduced to Europe by the Moors in Spain. Also popular was the guitar, which likewise seems to have come from Spain. Keyboard instruments like the virginal and later the harpsichord were to be found in many homes, and almost everyone who knew

16. *The development of musical notation: first line, neumes and text of the tenth century; second line, neumes and letters, eleventh century; third line, neumes on a broken line, eleventh century; fourth line, neumes on four-line staff, twelfth and thirteenth centuries; fifth line, squared neumes on four-line staff, twelfth century; sixth line, notes on five-line staff, fourteenth and fifteenth centuries; seventh line, same piece as above, but using hollow notation, seventeenth century; eighth line, same melody in modern notation. However, the time values of the different notes are still uncertain; ninth line, same piece, as written today in ¾ meter. (New York Public Library)*

anything about music knew how to play the recorder, a wind instrument.

Composers from all the European countries wrote for these instruments, and both their music and the instruments themselves are now enjoying a revival of popularity, for amateurs at home as well as for professionals on the concert stage.

Sixteenth-century Italy was composed of a number of independent dukedoms, principalities, and papal states, so-called because they were under the authority of the pope. Among the many courts, not only in Italy, but throughout Europe, there was great rivalry for the services of painters, scientists, architects, engineers —and, of course, for skilled musicians. As the nobility presented more and more lavish entertainments, more and more musicians were needed. Composers wrote madrigals, as well as purely instrumental music, and the same composer would be expected to serve in a duke's private chapel and to write music for the court ballets.

Especially in Italy, and to a lesser degree in France, the nobles who encouraged music and the other arts were famous. The Medici, Este, Gonzaga, and Borgia families all had great reputations as patrons of the arts and protectors of artists. Although these families were actively involved in plotting against each other and did not stop at murder, they did encourage the growth of music. Unfortunately, their encouragement of musicians too often consisted of praise, which cost them nothing, instead of money. Many a famous composer or performer was barely able to live on the salary his noble patron gave him.

Nevertheless, opportunities for the musician to compose and perform music did now exist to an extent never known before. And it was also possible for a musician to reach a new music-loving public. For instance, the Italian organist and composer Girolamo Frescobaldi (1583–1643), who was appointed to St. Peter's Basilica in Rome, was so popular that his playing drew thousands of listeners. Frescobaldi was a pioneer, one of the first composers to write for a solo instrument, the organ. For many generations his theories of composition and his methods of writing one melody against another, as in fugues, had a great influence on organists, including Johann Sebastian Bach, who lived a hundred years later.

In Mantua, an Italian city-state whose name is familiar to us as the setting of Shakespeare's comedy *The Taming of the Shrew,* members of the Gonzaga family had ruled as dukes from 1328 on and had acquired a reputation as patrons of music and painting. Their treatment of the first great composer of the new form of art known as opera illustrates their generosity and their stinginess, their knowledge and their ignorance of the arts they subsidized.

Claudio Monteverdi (1567–1643)

Claudio Giovanni Antonio Monteverdi was born in Cremona, a city renowned since about 1564 for the fine violins designed and built first by the Amati family, and later by their students, the Guarneri and Stradivari families. These Cremona violins, dating from the mid-sixteenth to the mid eighteenth centuries, are still considered the finest ever made.

Monteverdi's musical talents were recognized by his family when he was a child, and his father, a well-to-do physician, gave young Claudio a good education, including a fine musical training. While still in his teens, Monteverdi had already composed several madrigals. When he was about twenty, he set out to find a position as a musician. In 1590, as there were few professional opportunities for him in Cremona, he became a violist in the orchestra at the court of Mantua. The ruling Duke of Mantua had almost complete control of the lives of his subjects. He also had a passion for music and was fond enough of Monteverdi to let him marry. He even paid him the doubtful honor of taking him along to Hungary when Mantua waged an unsuccessful war against the Turks. Fortunately, Monteverdi returned unharmed.

However, Monteverdi was not happy in the duke's service. Time

17. Claudio Monteverdi. La Scala Museum. (Courtesy Italian Government Travel Office)

and again the duke passed him by when important and well-paying vacancies appeared among his court positions. Monteverdi received only minor promotions, and he complained bitterly both of his low salary and of the fact that his journeys with the duke had reduced him and his family almost to the point of starvation. By this time, he had two sons, and he needed more money to live on.

During this period of his life, Monteverdi composed many madrigals, and only later, when he finally became master of the chapel, responsible for the music in the duke's private chapel, did he start to write major religious compositions, such as Masses.

At the beginning of the seventeenth century, a group of poets in Florence had invented a new form of art that they first called the *new music,* and then *opera,* which is simply the Italian word for work, or deed. Their aims were to bring back to the stage what they believed to be the ideals and style of ancient

18. Jacopo Peri, composer of the first opera, in costume as Orfeo for a performance of his opera Euridice. La Scala Museum. *(Courtesy Italian Government Travel Office)*

Greek drama and music. The very first opera, *Dafne,* with music by Jacopo Peri, has mainly historical interest. But these Florentine musicians and poets had hit on a type of composition that turned out to be highly popular and was destined to reach musical heights they never dreamed of.

Monteverdi not only helped the new art form to become successful; he was able, because of his own musical genius, to change its direction. In 1607, his wife died, and his grief made it very difficult to concentrate on musical composition. But his children required food and care, and music was the only way he knew to earn a living. In the year of her death, he wrote his first opera, *Orfeo*. The performance was so successful that, when a marriage was arranged for the duke's heir, Monteverdi was ordered to produce a new opera for the occasion. He wrote *Arianna*, set to the words of Ottavio Rinuccini, the librettist of *Dafne*. Monteverdi was looking forward to a triumphant performance, when the young girl who was to sing the leading role fell sick of smallpox and died.

Eventually a new singer was chosen and the opera was performed. Monteverdi had composed music that expressed his own feeling of loss and sorrow at the death of his wife, and the beauty and sadness of one song, *Arianna's Lament,* were so intense that many members of the audience were moved to tears. Although the entire score of *Orfeo* has survived, only a few fragments of *Arianna* have been found. However, these fragments include the *Lament,* and modern audiences, too, are moved by this beautiful and tragic aria.

Even this success brought some disappointment, for Monteverdi was not paid the full fee promised him by the duke. The duke was always late in paying his captive genius of a composer, and he never paid all that he had promised.

In 1612, Duke Vicenzo died and was succeeded by the man for whose wedding Monteverdi had written *Arianna*. The first act of gratitude of the new duke was to fire Monteverdi. For a year, the renowned though unemployed composer found whatever musical jobs he could. Then, quite unexpectedly, he was offered the position of master of the chapel of San Marco Cathedral in Venice at a fine salary. For the first time in his life he felt financially secure. He plunged into his new work with great energy. He reorganized the chorus of the chapel, taught a number of aspiring musicians, and wrote many new religious works, including *Vespers* and *Glorias.* For three years he was kept so busy that he had no time to write new operas. His life was not dull, however. In Monteverdi's time, travel between cities had its hazards, and on one of his journeys from his home town of Cremona to Venice, he was held up and robbed by a highwayman.

19. *A ball in seventeenth-century Venice. A string trio at left supplies the* music. *From* Costumes of Men and Women, 1676. (*Courtesy Folger Shakespeare Library*)

According to a letter Monteverdi wrote about his experience, however, the highwayman was most polite and courteous.

The success of *Arianna* and the fame that his work in Venice brought him led to his receiving commissions from courts as far away as Poland. Even the Gonzagas of Mantua recognized their mistake and asked him to compose operas for their court. He did, and, as a free musician, this time he demanded and received a good fee.

Monteverdi's output in Venice was amazing. Although he was never really well during his stay in the damp City of Canals, he wrote religious Masses, operas, ballets, and madrigals seemingly without end.

His sons were now grown, one of them having become a priest, the other a doctor. But Italy, though it enjoyed the spirit of the Renaissance, was still subject to the tyranny of the Inquisition, a special religious body set up to ferret out heretical or un-authorized thoughts, and young Dr. Monteverdi was arrested for possessing a forbidden book. The composer wrote letters in his son's behalf, appealed to powerful friends, and raised money to free him. Despite all this, Monteverdi's faith in the Church was never shaken, and in 1632 he himself was ordained a priest.

Monteverdi influenced the entire history of musical drama. His operas were so successful and the Venetian public was so en-thusiastic about them that other composers were attracted to the new art, and a theater was opened for the sole purpose of produc-ing opera. This first opera house was soon followed by others. For the first time, the general public could purchase tickets to see and hear the musical spectacles that had previously been the personal amusement of the nobility.

After Monteverdi's death, Mantua was invaded and sacked, Venice was afflicted by a severe plague, and much of Italy was looted and burned time and again. In these disasters, many of Monteverdi's works disappeared. Enough survive, however, to con-vince us of his genius in the writing of melodies and of his technical skill in handling the orchestra. For about two hundred years, Monteverdi's name was almost completely forgotten by music historians, performers, and public. The present time has seen a revival of his fame, and concert performances of his *Orfeo, The Coronation of Poppea,* and other works are not infrequent.

IV

THE BAROQUE PERIOD

The art of composition, which had developed so slowly during the Middle Ages and then changed rapidly during the furiously active days of the Renaissance, was now changing more rapidly than ever. Composers were still learning how to write new kinds of music. As they realized what the human voice and the new instruments could do, they began to write increasingly complicated melodies. The heavily ornamented music that developed from the music of the Renaissance is now known as "baroque," and the term is applied to much of the music of the sixteenth and seventeenth centuries.

It should be understood that the terms *Renaissance* and *baroque* were names given to the music by critics and historians of a period long after the composers of that day were dead. Neither Frescobaldi nor the musicians who preceded or followed him knew that they were writing Renaissance or baroque music. They were simply writing the way they had learned from their teachers and from their own musical experiences.

ITALY

Monteverdi helped create the technique of modern musical composition. He was, to take but one example, the first composer to use the tremolo for string instruments—a simple device indeed, for it consisted of nothing but the rapid repetition of a single note. But this repetition by the strings, like a steady buzz or shimmer, lent an air of excitement to the entire orchestra as it accompanied a single voice singing a melody.

Orchestral instruments were still imperfect, and as instrument makers made one change after the other, composers took advantage of their improvements. Arcangelo Corelli (1653–1713) was the first important composer to write for the violin, which had newly developed from the old *vielle*. The violin, with its singing tone, was the first instrument that could be said to rival the human voice. However, it was not limited, as the voice was, to the production of single tones within a range of two or three octaves, and the player's fingers could produce notes more rapidly than any vocal chords. Students came to Corelli from all over Europe to learn how to write and play for the new instrument.

The insatiable demand for new operas opened up opportunities for dozens of composers. At one time there were seventeen opera houses in Venice alone, and hundreds throughout Italy. Opera was an exciting spectacle, filled with stunning stage effects. It combined the virtues we now find in moving pictures, the circus, and television. At the height of its popularity, it used up all the music that composers could supply. That was one reason why composers wrote so rapidly, turning out the music for a complete opera in two or three weeks. They worked under great pressure, as they usually had to copy all the parts for the orchestra themselves. The orchestra of that time was much smaller and less complicated than the modern orchestra, but writing out the parts still took time, as did the composition of new arias, overtures, and ballets.

No wonder that many composers often repeated themselves, borrowing bits and pieces from earlier works, and sometimes from works by others.

The composers who wrote for ballet and other forms of dance likewise found good markets for their musical wares. Peasant dances, with their strong, hearty rhythms, became the basis of the new purely instrumental music. Corelli and other composers for the violin developed the *suite,* a series of dances. In the suite, each dance was followed by another with a contrasting rhythm, to be played at a different speed, and with a different emotional effect.

Another famous Italian violinist of the baroque era was Giuseppe Tartini (1692–1770), a member of the nobility, who was equally renowned as fencer and violinist. Tartini was educated for careers in the army, the law, and the Church, and for a time seemed to have chosen the last. However, he fell in love and married, and that ended his career in the Church. Forced to flee from an angry cardinal, the uncle, or guardian, of his bride, he disguised himself as a monk and found sanctuary in a monastery at Assisi. Here he composed music and made improvements on the violin and bow. His *Devil's Trill Sonata*, which came to him in a dream, became a showpiece in his own lifetime and is still in the repertoire of every concert violinist. When his disguise was finally penetrated, his mastery of the violin brought him not only forgiveness for his offenses against the Church, but honor and international recognition, as well as reunion with his wife.

20. *Giuseppe Tartini.* (*New York Public Library*)

Antonio Vivaldi (c. 1675–1741)

Although it is more than two centuries since Antonio Vivaldi died, his musical reputation is still growing. Now highly regarded for his beautiful concertos, Vivaldi was also a composer of numerous operas. He wrote at great speed—one of his operas, it is said, taking him only five days. Once, when he was in an especially great hurry, he combined excerpts from operas by several other composers and passed the result off as his own.

21. *Virgin surrounded by musical angels. The angels are playing a curved horn, a recorder, and a viola da gamba (leg viol); sixteenth-century engraving by Jan Sadeler I. (Courtesy Metropolitan Museum of Art, Dick Fund, 1953)*

Vivaldi lived a peaceful life. Although he was ordained a priest, ill health saved him from being sent on any of the exhausting missions that other priests had to undertake. Instead, he was appointed musician priest to a conservatory for orphan girls in Venice. This institution, both home and school for the children who attended it, placed its emphasis on music.

Nothing could have better suited the calm, peaceful, and good-natured temperament of Vivaldi, who soon became known affectionately as the Red-Headed Priest. He composed religious services for the school and conducted its orchestra, for which he also composed concertos and sonatas. In this quiet and unaggressive way, he achieved an international reputation and soon received requests to compose operas and instrumental works for performance in other cities and other countries. By this time his health was good enough to let him travel and attend some of these performances in person.

Vivaldi was one of the first composers to write concertos for solo instruments. He was also one of the first to give some of his instrumental compositions descriptive titles. A group of four concertos known as *The Four Seasons* is especially delightful and popular. These and other concertos helped make the instrumental soloist an important personality.

Vivaldi's compositions had a great influence on his slightly younger contemporary, Johann Sebastian Bach. Bach rearranged many of Vivaldi's violin concertos and consciously used the musical devices he had learned from the Red-Headed Priest. In this way, though Vivaldi and even Bach were for a time forgotten, the two masters influenced the future development of orchestral music.

The Scarlattis

Musical talent often runs in families, and there are cases where generation after generation of one family has produced professional musicians. One such case is that of the Scarlatti family,

22. *Alessandro Scarlatti.* (*New York Public Library*)

in which Alessandro Scarlatti and his son Domenico were out-standing.

Alessandro Scarlatti (1660–1725) had a brother who was also a musician and a sister who was a singer. When the sister was not singing, however, she acquired so scandalous a reputation that she was ordered to enter a convent. Alessandro himself showed his musical talents at an early age. While he was still a young man, an opera of his attracted the interest of Queen Christina of Sweden, who was then living in Rome. Her patronage brought him to the attention of the public, and he became known throughout Italy. A few years later, he went to Naples as musical director of the Spanish viceroy's court there.

Scarlatti had other noble patrons after the viceroy. Although they were charmed by his music and lavish in their praise, they were usually slow in paying his fees. One nobleman, who owed Alessandro a fairly large sum, listened sympathetically to his plea for money to keep his wife and children from starving, and then said, still sympathetically, "I shall pray for you."

Alessandro was rescued from starvation, not by the generosity of his patrons, but by his talent for writing opera. The audiences of Naples demanded operas that had many brilliant and flowery passages in which the singers could display their beautiful voices and technical ability. They did not mind silly or absurd plots so long as the music held their interest.

Alessandro gave them the kind of operas they wanted, but he

IN DVE SEMBIANTI VN SOLO AMANTE ADORO

23. *The cover of the score of an opera by Alessandro Scarlatti.* (*Courtesy Library of Congress*)

also gave them such charming and beautiful music that he became for a time the most popular composer in Naples. Later, when
he moved back to Rome, he wrote in a different style, making
fewer concessions to star singers, and expressing more emotion
in the music itself.

While his music was popular, Alessandro was able to support
his family well enough, but he knew that audiences were fickle,
and what pleased them one day might not please them the next.
Even if an audience seemed loyal, he might lose his position with
the management of an opera house because of behind-the-scenes
intrigues of rival musicians.

Because of the constant threat of poverty, Alessandro set his
children to work as soon as possible. In his son Domenico (1685–
1757), the sixth child of ten, Alessandro quickly found that he
had a genius. Alessandro knew important people in Naples, and
although they were not always inclined to help him, apparently
they did have a hand in getting Domenico a position as composer
and organist in the Royal Chapel in Naples.

24. *Domenico Scarlatti.*
(*New York Public Library*)

It did not take much time for Domenico Scarlatti to win recognition as the best harpsichordist of his day. He was not quite the greatest organist. At the age of twenty-four, he took part in an organ competition with Handel, who was then in Rome, and he himself confessed that Handel was master of that instrument. Handel returned the compliment by acknowledging Domenico's prowess on the harpsichord. Despite the competition, the two young men respected each other and became good friends.

When a good offer came along from a Portuguese prince, Domenico accepted it. Later, in the service of the same royal patron, he went to Spain, where he spent most of the rest of his life. His years in Spain left their echoes in his music, and we can hear the strumming of guitars and the strong rhythms of Spanish dances in many of his sonatas for the harpsichord.

Thanks to his father's help at the beginning of his career, Domenico was more successful in making money than his father had been. Unfortunately, he had an incurable passion for gambling, and his losses often reduced his family to poverty.

Domenico was familiar with the piano, which had been invented around 1709 by Bartolomeo Cristofori (1655–1731), an Italian instrument maker. However, he did not like the tone or action of the crude piano of his day, and his numerous sonatas were written for the harpsichord. Today, they are performed more frequently on the modern piano than on the harpsichord.

For two centuries, the compositions of his father, Alessandro, remained almost forgotten. Now some of the music from Alessandro's more than a hundred operas is being revived and recorded, along with his chamber music and some of his more than five hundred religious compositions. Modern audiences find in the music of both father and son the same charm and grace that appealed to the music-loving audiences of their own day.

Few operas of the baroque period are performed today, despite the lovely music they may contain. Modern audiences cannot identify with the mythical characters who are involved in endless plots with gods and goddesses. Also, many of the female roles, as well as some male roles, were written for *castrati*, male singers with female voices. The range and quality of the music often do not suit either the contralto or tenor voices of today.

ENGLAND

Henry VIII, King of England in the early sixteenth century, was a musical monarch. Henry played several instruments—all of them, according to a contemporary writer, like an accomplished musician. His daughter, Elizabeth, who later became queen, was also vain of her ability to play several instruments. She was especially skillful on the virginal, an early form of piano.

Henry and Elizabeth ruled a musical nation. In every castle, village, and hamlet, rich and poor sang, danced, and played musical instruments. This was so, not only during the Renaissance, but for almost a century after the death of Elizabeth. Keyboard instruments such as the virginal and the harpsichord became popular with those who could afford them, but the most important instrument remained the human voice. The ability to sing and play became the mark of an educated man.

While the amateur musicians flourished, so did the professionals. They composed madrigals, wrote music for masques, which com-

25. *Music in England, 1628. A singer, viol player, and virginalist.* (*Courtesy Folger Shakespeare Library*)

bined singing, dancing, and spectacular pageantry, and adapted English folk tunes to formal compositions.

In 1532 Henry VIII had both personal and political problems. A man of many wives, he had married his first wife, Catherine of Aragon, for political reasons, and now wished to divorce her in order to marry Anne Boleyn. In Rome, however, the pope refused to grant him a divorce, while in England, Henry found himself short of money and surrounded by political enemies. Henry solved all his difficulties at once by breaking with the pope, seizing the properties of the Catholic Church in England, and putting himself at the head of a newly established Anglican Church, to which all loyal Englishmen were expected to belong. As head of the church, Henry gave himself a divorce, blessed his own marriage to Anne Boleyn, and used the church's property as he pleased.

The new church needed a new ritual, along with new music, and Henry looked for gifted composers to supply it. Thomas Tallis (c. 1505–85) was one of the men he chose. Tallis had been an organist in a Catholic monastery, but Henry did not hold this against him. Nor did his daughter, Elizabeth, when she came to the throne. Elizabeth appointed Tallis and his pupil, William Byrd (c. 1543–1623), to be joint organists in the Royal Chapel. Byrd was a lifelong Catholic.

The Elizabethan Age gave to the world such master playwrights as Shakespeare, Christopher Marlowe, and Ben Jonson. Science was beginning to flourish, and London, the political and cultural center of England, had also become a thriving commercial city. Musicians could find work everywhere, playing incidental music to serious plays, and composing dance tunes and interludes.

In 1649, less than half a century after Elizabeth's death, Oliver Cromwell and the Puritans he led overthrew and beheaded Charles I, and England entered a new era in which it was called the Commonwealth.

The Puritans have been blamed for the sorry state of musical composition in England since their time, and the word "Puritan" has become to many people a synonym for "bluenose" or "kill-joy." The faults of the Puritans have been greatly exaggerated. It is true that some of the more ignorant and bigoted among them not only closed theaters but banned all formal church music and, to make sure that religious services would not be too musical, destroyed church organs and burned books of church music. During this same period of the Commonwealth, however, more music was published in England than ever before.

Cromwell himself was so fond of music that he paid his daughter's music teacher a hundred pounds a year for lessons—a considerable sum for those days. He is even supposed to have pardoned a royalist because the man played the violin so well. During this period, Italian opera, almost certainly written by Catholic composers, was introduced to England. The composer Matthew Locke wrote a masque called *Cupid and Death*, hardly the kind of title we now associate with Puritanism. It was given an official performance by the government in honor of a foreign diplomat.

John Milton, the poet, was the son of a musician and a fine musician himself—and at the same time a Puritan. Another famous Puritan, John Bunyan, the author of *Pilgrim's Progress*, was also a lover of music.

The absurdity of blaming the Puritans for the death of English music becomes obvious when we realize that the greatest English composer did his work *after* their rule was ended.

Henry Purcell (c. 1659–95)

Although Henry Purcell, after three centuries, is still considered England's greatest native-born composer, we know all too little about him. We are still unsure of the year he was born, and which of two brothers was his father. We do know that he was born in London about the time Cromwell died, and that he received his musical training from his father. As a young child he became a singer in the Royal Chapel, where he received an allowance of thirty pounds a year, as well as an education. The young choristers were given highly elaborate and decorative scar-

26. Henry Purcell. (Courtesy Trustees of the British Museum)

let costumes adorned with silk lace, but by Purcell's time, the scarlet had become dull with dirt, the lace had torn, and the children often looked like ragamuffins.

While still a young boy, Purcell appears to have written a number of anthems, which are religious compositions. At the age of fourteen his voice changed, but he was allowed to continue at the chapel as a student and an apprentice instrument maker and repairer. In Purcell's day, it was often necessary for professional musicians to make or repair their own instruments, and the tradition has, to some extent, continued to the present time.

Purcell studied with composers and teachers who were associated with the chapel, and possibly with John Blow (c. 1648–1708), who was not only a prominent composer, but a kind and self-sacrificing man. To earn a living, Purcell became a copyist. As printed music was still expensive, it was often necessary—as it still is at times today—to copy all the parts of a score by hand. This was tedious work, but it gave the young copyist an opportunity to become acquainted with the music of many composers.

At the age of eighteen or nineteen, Purcell was appointed composer for the orchestra of the new king, Charles II. While the Puritans were in power, Charles had spent the years of his exile in France, had become very fond of the music he heard there, and expected his own composers to write in a similar manner. One of Purcell's music teachers had been trained in France and Italy, and from him Purcell learned how to write in both the French and Italian styles. Purcell's own personality and creative ability were so outstanding, however, that he never became a mere imitator.

Purcell also wrote a considerable amount of incidental music for the theater. A writer called Shadwell concocted inferior but successful adaptations of Shakespeare's plays, and Purcell composed music for them as well as for plays by John Dryden and William Congreve.

In 1689, John Blow resigned as organist at Westminster Abbey so that Purcell might get the position, with its salary of ten pounds a year and an allowance of eight pounds for the rent of a house. At this time Purcell was still composer for the Royal Chapel orchestra. Two years later he was appointed organist of the Royal Chapel, and, still later, keeper of the king's musical instruments. Throughout this period he was also writing sonatas, fantasias, anthems, and operas.

He had become busy and famous but still not very successful financially. His combined salaries were barely enough to support a wife and two children, and did not compare with the hundred pounds that Cromwell gave his daughter's music teacher. To make matters worse, very often the money due him was not paid promptly or in full.

In 1689, he almost lost his position at the abbey because he collected fees for seating spectators in the organ loft at the coronation of a new pair of rulers, William and Mary. Purcell apparently considered these fees as part of the income due him, but the authorities of the abbey threatened him with immediate dismissal unless he turned the money over to them. We do not know the details of what followed, but it appears that Purcell yielded and gave them the money, for he was not fired.

In addition to his many compositions for religious services, coronations, ballets, and masques, Purcell wrote a number of operas of which his most famous is *Dido and Aeneas.* As no opera house management would risk the production of an opera by a native composer, it was first performed at a girls' school. An aria, "I Attempt from Love's Sickness to Fly," one of the most beautiful songs ever written, is from another of his operas, *The Indian Queen.*

Working steadily to turn out music and to support his family, Purcell became ill and died at the age of thirty-six. By this time his international reputation was so great that the Italian composer Corelli had been planning a trip to England just to meet him. Once Purcell was dead, however, even his own countrymen appreciated him, and he was buried with many honors in that same Westminster Abbey whose authorities had harassed him while he was still alive.

His son, Edward, later became a well-known organist but lacked the genius of his father. English music went downhill after Purcell's death, and for the next two hundred years, with minor exceptions, Merrie England had to depend for its musical life on foreign visitors.

FRANCE

During the Renaissance, France became one of the most powerful countries of Europe, and its capital, Paris, attracted many writers, artists, philosophers, and musicians. Some settled in Paris to live; others spent several years there, to profit from the intellectual and emotional stimulation for which the great city was famous.

Artistic and intellectual influence worked both ways, and if Paris stimulated visiting Italians, Germans, Spaniards, Hollanders, and Englishmen, it was in turn stimulated by them. Such noted visitors as Leonardo da Vinci and Erasmus, the philosopher, could hardly have failed to leave the imprint of their genius.

Ballet was an Italian import, but the French very soon made it

27. *The joys of music in France. Viols, bass, and a harpsichord are shown.* (*Courtesy Library of Congress*)

their own, and no musical program stood much chance of success unless it included a ballet. Italian opera was introduced about 1645 and caught on immediately—once ballets were added to it. By the time of Louis XIV (1638–1715), French musical life had become very active. It owed most of its activity, however, to an Italian immigrant, Giovanni Battista Lulli.

Jean Baptiste Lully (1632–87)

All his life, Giovanni Lulli was shrewd, talented, and skilled at looking out for his own interests. At an early age, his ability to play the guitar impressed the Chevalier de Guise, a French nobleman who was visiting Florence, and De Guise took the young street urchin to France. As his own family was poor, and Giovanni faced a bleak future at home, his parents were delighted to accept

28. *A scene from* Atys, *an opera by Lully. From a contemporary engraving.* (*Courtesy French Cultural Services*)

29. *Jean Baptiste Lully.* (*Courtesy French Cultural Services*)

the money that the chevalier offered as compensation for the loss
of Giovanni's future earnings.

Lulli was presented by the Chevalier de Guise to a female
cousin at the French court, and she, unimpressed by either his
talent or his appearance, at once put the boy to work in her
kitchen. In the same quick, almost miraculous manner in which
he had somehow learned to play the guitar, young Lulli also
learned to play the violin. His playing was soon overheard by a

count, who seems to have said to Lulli's owner, "That's a talented boy you have there." Impressed by the count's discernment, the lady transferred Lulli from the kitchen to her private orchestra.

Here he did well until she heard an unpleasant song he had written about her, and immediately threw him out of her home.

By this time, however, his talents had come to the attention of King Louis himself. The king hired him as a member of the royal orchestra, and Lulli's swift rise began. He was promoted a number of times, and eventually received from the king special rights that gave him practically a monopoly on all musical performances in France. Somewhere along the way he changed his name to its French form of Jean Baptiste Lully.

In the writing of operas (complete with ballets) and the composition of instrumental works, no one at the French court could compete with him. Court dancing had tended to be slow and stately, but Lully changed that by introducing lively music, to which he danced himself, as did the king. Lully introduced new instruments into the orchestra and devised new orchestral techniques. He also raised the level of orchestral discipline. When he gave the beat, *all* his musicians followed it. The contrast with the sloppy, slightly-out-of-tune orchestras of most other courts was striking. As an autocrat with the power of the king behind him, Lully exercised the firmest musical discipline with his players.

It is said that power corrupts, but Lully seems to have been corrupted even before he attained his great power. He was greedy, treacherous, and an associate of vicious individuals. His better side was reserved for his music, in which he showed such taste and ability that he influenced most of the musicians in Southern Europe.

He collaborated with such well-known playwrights as Molière and Quinault, and all through his life he made an endless study of music and aimed to become proficient on all instruments. He still found time to amass a tremendous fortune, chiefly because of his musical monopoly, and to attain additional security by marrying a wealthy girl. The king honored him as no one outside the nobility had ever before been honored, and Lully became so

30. Jean Philippe Rameau. (Courtesy French Cultural Services)

puffed up about his own genius that he invented tales of his own noble birth.

His death resulted from an accident incurred while conducting. In those days, a composer was usually his own conductor, and would lead the orchestra from the harpsichord or some other instrument. At other times he gave the beat by standing before the orchestra and pounding on the floor with a long, heavy stick. This was what Lully was doing when he struck his own foot. Infection developed, and death followed after treatment by the murderous medical methods then in vogue.

French music continued to flourish after Lully's death. Jean Philippe Rameau (1683–1764), who wrote over twenty operas, as well as much harpsichord music, introduced further changes in the use of musical instruments. And François Couperin (1668–1733), known as le Grand, or the Great, to distinguish him from the many other members of his highly musical family, was one of the pioneers in improving keyboard music and technique.

The last influential composer in the history of French music during this period was also not a native Frenchman, but an Austrian whose musical education was largely Italian.

Christoph Willibald Gluck (*1714–87*)

Christoph Gluck composed for more than twenty years and acquired an international reputation by writing music with which he himself became increasingly dissatisfied. It was only when he discarded his old methods and began to write in a new way that he composed the music that would assure him a place among the immortals.

Born in Bavaria, he studied music in the local Jesuit seminary, and then went to Prague, where he continued his studies and supported himself—as countless other musicians have done—by giving lessons. In the summer he picked up a bit of extra money by playing polkas and peasant waltzes for villages near the city. After

31. Christoph Willibald Gluck. (Courtesy German Information Center)

four years in Prague, he went to Vienna, where he found a patron, Prince Melzi. As patrons went in those days, the prince was an excellent one. He took Gluck with him on a trip to Italy, and in Milan arranged for the young musician to study with a prominent composer and teacher, Giovanni Battista Sammartini (1701–75).

In the prince's service, Gluck composed eight operas which were well received. As a result of their success, Gluck was invited to compose operas for the King of England at the Haymarket Theatre in London.

The result was disastrous. English audiences had no great liking for the elaborate imitation Italian operas that Gluck composed, and they were complete failures. The English preferred authentic Italian operas or the operas of Handel.

Gluck was not a man to be crushed by defeat. He composed and performed a concerto for drinking glasses, tuned with spring water. Although this unusual instrument attracted a fairly large audience, it was the kind of audience he himself would later despise.

The drinking-glass concerto did not endear him to Handel, who was then living in London. Handel said contemptuously that Gluck knew no more about counterpoint than his cook.

On his way back from London, Gluck stopped off in Paris to hear the operas popular in France. He was greatly impressed by the work of Rameau, who wrote in a simple style very different from that of the Italian composers. Gluck's unhappy experience in London had caused him to ask himself a number of difficult questions, to which the work of Rameau gave some idea of the answer.

When a composer writes an opera, is he interested chiefly in the money he hopes to make, or does he have loftier motives? What should an opera *be*? Certainly not a showpiece for a group of vain singers, such as Gluck had been writing in his drive for success.

Gluck returned to Vienna and resumed his career as a composer of the kind of opera the public expected of him. He was attached to the Austrian court where, among other duties, he taught music to Marie Antoinette, later to become Queen of France and to lose her head during the French Revolution. In Vienna he was attracted to a wealthy young woman whose banker father violently opposed their marriage. Gluck was a musician, he lived a vagabond life, and a face marked by the scars of smallpox gave him an unprepossessing appearance. What sane, wealthy young Viennese girl would want him for a husband?

These arguments failed to sway the girl, but whatever she felt, her father—for a time—had the last word. Gluck went to Rome, to work on his operas and forget. After a year, however, the girl's father died, and Gluck hastened back to Vienna to marry his fiancée. The marriage was a happy one.

Later he returned to Rome and was knighted by the pope. The knighthood entitled Gluck to call himself the Chevalier *von* Gluck, the *von* being a sign of nobility. Gluck proudly adopted the new form of his name.

All through these years, he was writing one kind of opera and thinking of another. By 1762, however, assisted by the libretto and by the ideas of an Italian poet, Raniero da Calzabigi, he had written the music for *Orfeo ed Euridice* (*Orpheus and Euryd-ice*), an opera in his revolutionary new style. This achieved only a fair success in Vienna, although two operas he wrote after that did better. But in Paris, after great opposition by those who favored Italian opera, a French version of *Orfeo ed Euridice* was a hit.

What was so revolutionary about his new style? In opera, Gluck wrote, music should assist the poetic expression, touch the hearts of the audience, and help to tell the story. Every note written merely to satisfy the vanity of a singer should be mercilessly cut out, and so should every repetition of an aria that slowed the action and made the audience forget the story.

Gluck's approach was a logical one, but logic had no appeal for people who had come to regard an opera as a series of recitals in costume by the different singers. Gluck's enemies in Paris united against him, and even imported a then famous Italian composer, Nicola Piccini (1728–1800), to lead the attack against him. Gluck eventually won, and Piccini was a better man than the people he led, for he admitted later that he admired Gluck's work.

The years of battle against hostile musicians and audiences exhausted Gluck, and he returned to Vienna to live out the eight years still remaining to him.

Plagued by ill health, he kept up his interest in music, although he himself was no longer able to compose. He became an admirer of the work of the young Mozart, and it must have amused him to learn that Mozart too wrote a composition for musical glasses. He died of a stroke on November 15, 1787.

Thanks to the beauty of its music, his opera *Orfeo ed Euridice* was the first to remain in the repertory of all major opera companies.

GERMANY

In Italy and France, the Renaissance was a time of rapid artistic and cultural change, accompanied by war and political upheaval. In Germany, the Reformation, brought about by Martin Luther in the early sixteenth century, made the Renaissance a period of religious conflict as well.

It was a difficult time to survive, let alone to compose music. Thanks to Richard Wagner's opera *Die Meistersinger von Nürnberg,* many of us have heard of the mastersingers, as they were called in English. Wagner's picture of them is accurate but one-sided. The mastersingers were middle-class descendants of the old *minnesingers,* or love singers, who were contemporaries of the troubadours. They were organized into guilds, and they did hold prize competitions, as Wagner describes. But the chief reason that a guild was formed, whether its members were musicians or locksmiths, was to protect their interests and to make sure that no nonguild musician took away the job of a guild member.

Wagner's all-knowing character, Hans Sachs, actually existed and wrote thousands of musical compositions. Sachs and other mastersingers were strong supporters of Martin Luther and wrote hymns for the new Lutheran Church, many of them based on folk tunes sung by the peasants.

32. *Emperor Maximilian I, of Germany, visiting a music store. Note the drums, trombone, horns on the right, the harp in the center, and organ to the left. From a fifteenth-century woodcut. (Courtesy Austrian Institute in New York)*

,bie krieget mit fange K walth' voɔ vogtlweiɔe · lj wolfran von Grchalbach.
h'Rennander Alte ɔer tugenthafte Schuber hemrich vo Oſterninge
vñ klingeſoɽ von vñgerlant.

33. *A group of minnesingers at a musical congress, twelfth century.* (*New York Public Library*)

A few members of the nobility invited composers of the Netherlands and Italian schools to write music for their courts and chapels, but their music remained unknown to the rising new middle classes, and to the middle-class mastersingers. None of the German composers who lived in Luther's time achieved lasting fame. After Luther's death, the walls separating the different kinds of music—church, concert, mastersinger, and folk song— might have been broken down if not for the Thirty Years' War, which from 1618 on swept over all Europe and disrupted the lives of all classes. The thirty years of chaos had an especially disastrous effect in Germany, where many of the battles took place.

Because of the devastation and hopelessness of daily life, many people turned more to religion, which promised them a better future. German music became primarily religious, and German musicians became known for their organ playing for church services. Most of the composers of this time wrote Lutheran chorales, in which they made use of counterpoint and other musical devices that had been invented and improved by composers of other lands.

The leading German composer of the seventeenth century, Heinrich Schütz (1585–1672), was born before the Thirty Years' War started, and lived for almost twenty-five years after it ended. After studying in Italy, he returned to Germany and became composer for the Elector of Saxony, as the ruler of this German state was called. The time not occupied in composing and conducting was spent in desperate moves from one place in Germany to another, and even to Scandinavia, in an effort to avoid the dozens of bandit armies that ravaged the country in the name of religion.

Johann Sebastian Bach (1685–1750)

Even in the worst days of the Thirty Years' War, one family of musicians managed not only to survive but to pass on its skills from generation to generation. The name of the family, *Bach,* is the German word for *brook,* and it is interesting to note how the Bachs flowed on and contributed to each other's education. The family was so large and its members so devoted to each other that they held annual reunions. All were professional musicians employed in widely scattered cities and churches. The one day a year on which the Bachs met was spent in eating, talking, playing, and singing. On this day, as always, the Bachs thought, spoke, and breathed music.

Even their humor was musical. A favorite diversion was the *quodlibet,* or *what you please,* in which each participant played or sang any words or music he thought of or remembered, without regard to melody, harmony, or rhythm. The effect was often that of bedlam, although skillful musicians might actually manage to sing in harmony with snatches of different compositions sung by their fellows.

Into this family, Johann Sebastian Bach, who belonged to the fifth known generation of musicians, was born in the town of

34. An orchestral performance in an eighteenth-century German church. Note the shape of the viols' bows. (New York Public Library)

Eisenach, Germany. At a very early age, he began to take lessons
from his father and showed the talent that was to be expected
from a Bach. His father died when Johann Sebastian was ten,
and the orphan went to live with an older brother, who also gave
him music lessons.

His brother's income was barely sufficient to support a wife and
growing family, and Johann Sebastian left at the age of fifteen.
Because of his ability to sing, he was accepted by a school at a
convent in a nearby town and was assigned to the chorus. Fifteen,
however, is hardly the ideal age for a boy soprano. Bach's voice
soon began to change, and he was dropped from the chorus. Fortunately, he was a proficient violinist, and he was allowed to
stay on in the orchestra.

At the school he received a general education and must also
have learned to play the organ, for at eighteen he was organist in
the New Church in Arnstadt. He had begun to compose several
years before, and in Arnstadt he was able to devote more time to
composition.

At the same time, he continued to improve his skill as an
organist, and in October 1705, he asked for a leave of four weeks to
hear the famed Danish organist Dietrich Buxtehude (1637–1707)
in Lübeck. Leave was given grudgingly, and Bach walked the
fifty miles to Lübeck, listened to Buxtehude's inspired playing—
and for almost a half year forgot about going back. Not until
February 1706 did he return to his own job in the New Church.

The New Church authorities were furious and summoned him
to a disciplinary meeting, where they found a great deal of fault
with him. He could not discipline his choir; he lacked self-disci-
pline, as his long absence showed; and he was so quarrelsome that
he had been involved in a sword fight with another musician,
whose bassoon he had insulted. And as if all this were not bad
enough, he was charged with permitting a girl to sit in the church
loft. To this final charge, Bach pleaded guilty. The girl was not
only his fiancée, but his cousin as well, daughter of another musician in the Bach family, and Bach saw nothing wrong in let-
ting her sit in the church loft.

35. *Johann Sebastian Bach. (Courtesy German Information Center)*

The New Church authorities did not agree, and they made life so unpleasant for him that in 1707 he found a job as organist elsewhere and married his fiancée.

The new job was not satisfactory either, and Bach next became court organist and musician to the Duke of Weimar. Here, for eight years, he was able to live comfortably and compose for the duke's pleasure. But when an important position was open, and Bach was by-passed, he was so angry that he accepted a position with another nobleman, the Prince of Anhalt-Cöthen. The Duke of Weimar was furious with Bach for acting without his permission, and threw the composer into prison. After a month, however, the duke accepted the inevitable and let Bach go.

Bach's new patron, the Prince of Anhalt-Cöthen, was himself a good musician, and he treated his composer well, even taking him along on his travels.

It was while Bach was away on one such trip that his wife died. They had been married thirteen years and had had seven children, of whom four were living. Though Bach mourned the loss of his wife, he realized that he needed someone to take care of his children, and he soon married again.

Anna Magdalena, his second wife, was also the daughter of a musician. She was a fine singer and accompanist, but she must soon have had little time for singing and playing, for she not only took care of the children by Bach's first wife, but bore him thirteen children herself. It seems almost incredible that she was able to help Bach by copying music and teaching his children to copy music also.

Bach was happy in his work, happy in his second marriage as in his first, but unhappy about his children. Anhalt-Cöthen was a small town, and there were no good schools nearby. For the sake of his children—and partly for his own sake, for he missed working on an organ such as he would find in a large church—Bach once more looked for a new job.

Eventually he found it in St. Thomas's Church in Leipzig. Here he had to demonstrate his skill as organist and composer, but he passed both tests with ease and was appointed organist. Again

36. St. Thomas's Church in Leipzig, where Bach spent the latter part of his life. (Courtesy German Information Center)

he had difficulties with the church authorities, who were always trying to save money at his expense. But despite difficulties, it was in Leipzig that he stayed for the rest of his life, and it was in Leipzig that fame finally came to him.

During all the years of disagreements with church authorities and patrons, he had been turning out music in the form of fugues, suites, Masses, concertos, and chorales. He even found time to write a humorous vocal piece, the "Coffee Cantata," as an affectionate gesture to his wife, who loved to drink coffee.

Because of his skill as an organist, he was invited to churches and courts throughout Germany. His genius as a composer was not fully appreciated, perhaps because he never wrote operas, which would have ensured him wide public recognition. He was a very devout man, and his major religious works, such as the *Mass in B Minor* and *The Passion According to St. Matthew*, express the depth of his feelings in some of the most magnificent music ever written.

The years of writing and copying music may have weakened his eyes, which were none too strong to start with. Whatever the cause, he was beginning to lose his sight. An operation by a visiting surgeon from England blinded him completely, and a second operation failed to repair the damage done by the first. Before this, in a century when disease, helped along by ignorant physicians and surgeons, struck down almost half the population before the age of twenty, Bach had never suffered a serious illness in his life. The two eye operations, however, made him a complete invalid. But even from his sickbed, Bach continued to work, dictating music to one of his children or to a son-in-law. One morning he awoke and appeared to have recovered his sight again. Several days later, however, he suffered a stroke and died.

He was mourned by the musicians of Germany, but in other countries his death was hardly noted. The reason was simple: abroad, as at home, he was famous less as a composer than as a performer, a master organist with a marvelous ability to improvise. Those countries, like England, where he had never appeared, had little idea of what the world of music had lost. And in Germany itself, as in the rest of Europe, Bach's work was overshadowed during his lifetime by that of another composer.

37. *Wilhelm Friedemann Bach, the ne'er-do-well son of Johann Sebastian Bach. (Courtesy German Information Center)*

Georg Philipp Telemann (1681–1767)

An amazingly versatile man, Georg Philipp Telemann was not educated for a musical career. Not until he became a student of law, languages, and science at the University of Leipzig did he learn music by taking informal lessons on the organ and studying musical scores. He was so apt a student that he was appointed organist at the New Church in Leipzig while still at the university.

He soon realized that music offered the kind of career he wanted, and he spent the rest of his eighty-six years performing and composing. His output of musical compositions was so vast that he himself could not keep track of them. He composed a great deal of church music, about forty operas, as well as over six hundred orchestral overtures, directed the opera in Hamburg, conducted concerts, wrote his own librettos for his many choral compositions, and found time to write textbooks on music as well as several autobiographies.

He had the respect and friendship of the greatest musicians of his own generation. Handel once said admiringly that Telemann could write an eight-part motet as easily as anyone else could write a letter. Bach was a close friend of his, and Telemann was godfather of Bach's son Carl Philipp Emanuel.

Telemann was a man of broad culture and varied interests, and his ever-youthful spirit welcomed new trends in music, as in other arts. Those who objected to any changes in the musical *status quo* he regarded as fossils.

The music of both Telemann and Bach was slowly forgotten after their deaths. When interest in Bach's music was revived during the nineteenth century, Telemann's music suffered all the more, for now it was compared, to its detriment, with that of his great contemporary, and the critical verdict that it was "shallow" and showed a lack of inventiveness discouraged musicians from playing it.

In our own century, however, the availability of records and tapes of Telemann's compositions has won him a new audience, and critical opinion of his abilities as a composer is becoming more favorable.

The Younger Bachs

The sons of Johann Sebastian Bach were also talented composers, and their works became the object of much greater admiration and acclaim than the glorious compositions of their father had ever received.

Bach's youngest son, Johann Christian (1735–82), who converted to Catholicism, had a successful career in Naples as a composer of operas and, in Milan, as a church organist. He finally settled in London, where he became music master to the Queen of England. He married an opera singer, taught the young Mozart when the latter visited London, and lived a very fashionable life.

Bach's older sons, Wilhelm Friedemann (1710–84) and Carl Philipp Emanuel (1714–88), were also accomplished musicians. Friedemann, however, was not the sturdy, steady man his father had been. Perhaps he suffered from living in his father's shadow. He became an alcoholic, deserted his wife and child, and is also said to have plagiarized some of the music his father composed, because he was either too drunk or too lazy to write his own. Emanuel was more like his father, and worked for many years as a musician for Frederick the Great (1712–86), King of Prussia.

After Johann Sebastian, the Bach family produced two more generations of fine musicians and then seems to have disappeared from the history of music. Various reasons have been suggested. Perhaps the boys in the family never lived to maturity; perhaps the members of the family realized that, despite occasional exceptions, music did not pay. Johann Sebastian Bach died a poor man, and his widow, a good musician in her own right, lived in poverty for the ten years she survived him. His youngest daughter, left alone, was kept alive by a fund established by a few generous musicians and music lovers. Contributors to the fund included

38. Carl Philipp Emanuel Bach, another musician son of Johann Sebastian Bach. (Courtesy German Information Center)

Beethoven, among other composers. It did not include the authorities of St. Thomas's Church, whose sole claim to fame was that Bach worked there.

Whatever the reason, the third generation of Bachs after Johann Sebastian was not noted for its musicians.

George Frederic Handel (1685–1759)

George Frederic Handel was born in the city of Halle in the same golden year that saw the births of Domenico Scarlatti and Johann Sebastian Bach. He was a child prodigy who played the clavichord beautifully at the age of seven and was composing complicated music by the time he was eleven. His father, who was over sixty when George Frederic was born, was proud of his son's talent, but at the same time unhappy about it. Musicians were rarely accepted as respectable, honored members of the community; he would see to it that his son became a lawyer.

In deference to his father's wishes, George Frederic did study law for a time at the University of Halle, but soon gave it up. His talent was for music, and a musician he would be, no matter what hardships such a career might bring. His father died while he was still a boy, and his mother, more sympathetic to her son's love for music, permitted him to concentrate on music lessons and practice.

By the age of eighteen, Handel had become a fine musician and an excellent organist, but he realized that he still had much to learn. He went to Hamburg, which was then a musical and operatic center, and, thanks to the friendship of a singer-composer named Johann Mattheson (1681–1764), he found a job in an orchestra.

The great organist Buxtehude attracted them to Lübeck, as he had attracted Bach, and they were thrilled by his masterful performances. Buxtehude was planning to retire, and both Handel and Mattheson considered applying for his position. They discovered, however, that the work had an important nonmusical requirement: before an applicant could get the job, he would have to marry Buxtehude's daughter. The girl did not appeal to either of the two young men, who turned tail and ran for their lives. Eventually, the poor girl did snare a husband who became Buxtehude's successor.

Georges Frederic Schmidt Sculp. a Paris

GEORGES FREDERIC HANDEL
Seul Compositeur & Directeur General
de l'Opera de Londres
Né en Saxe.

39. *George Frederic Handel.* (*Courtesy Trustees of the British Museum*)

The friendship between Handel and Mattheson, at first very close, broke up because of professional rivalry. Each wanted the right to complete an operatic performance at the harpsichord, and neither would yield an inch. The result was a duel with swords, in which Handel escaped death when Mattheson's sword point broke off on a coat button.

Handel remained in Hamburg for several years, busily turning out operas, cantatas, and pieces for the clavichord. In 1706, however, a producer mutilated one of his operas by cutting out whole sections and inserting scenes of slapstick comedy. Handel was outraged, but there was nothing he could do about it. In disgust, he left Germany for what he hoped would be the better musical climate of Italy.

In Italy he met the Scarlatti family and other important composers. He also studied Italian music, listened to folk songs and dances, and acquired a passion for painting. One of his greatest pleasures was visiting art galleries. He himself posed for a number of portraits, which show him first as a serious-looking young man, neither handsome nor homely, and later as a heavy-set man in his middle age. The portraits indicate the warmth of his personality and his good humor.

Handel continued to write while in Italy. His compositions there were influenced by the Italian music he heard; they included operas, cantatas, and oratorios, the cantatas being performed in Venice and the oratorios in Rome.

While he was in Venice, he was invited to return to Germany as chapelmaster at the court of Hanover. Behind the invitation lay a curious story. The Elector of Hanover, it appeared, was so enamored of Italian opera that he spent more time in Venice than he did at home. To lure him back from Italy, his subjects had an opera house built in Hanover itself. This was not done, however, out of sheer affection for their ruler. In Italy, the elector spent enormous sums of money, went into debt, and paid his creditors with the cash he received from the sale of his subjects as mercenaries. It was to save their own skins that the citizens of Hanover wanted their duke to return.

Handel accepted the offer to come to Hanover, but he did not stay long. The English made him a better offer, and in 1710 he went to London on a leave of absence. From that year on, he spent most of his time in England, with an occasional visit to Hanover. When he first arrived in England, London was mad about Italian opera, and Handel was greeted warmly by both the queen and the producers of opera. Handel's own operas were a great success, and his music pleased the queen so greatly that he was appointed Composer to the Court.

While Handel was enjoying his English success, he forgot that he still had obligations to the Elector of Hanover. He was unpleasantly reminded in 1714, when the queen died, and the Elector of Hanover became King George I (1660–1727) of England.

Handel was not interested in politics, and he had at first no idea that his stay in England had been regarded by the elector as an act of hostility. When he did realize this, he tried to regain the king's favor by writing an opera for him. Another story has it that his reconciliation with the king resulted from his composition of an orchestral suite called *Water Music,* which Handel arranged to have played on the royal barge.

Whatever music deserved the credit, the reconciliation did take place. And if compositions were needed to please the king, Handel could provide them, for he now poured out vast quantities of music. He could write a concerto in a day, an opera in twenty days.

At this period in his life, everything was going well, with one important exception. Handel was receiving fees for his music, but

*40. "The Charming Brute,"
a contemporary English
caricature of Handel. (New
York Public Library)*

41. *A rehearsal of a Handel oratorio, as engraved by William Hogarth. (New York Public Library)*

it was the producers of his operas who were becoming rich, and not Handel. As he told one producer, "For the next opera, let's turn things around. You write it, and *I'll* produce it."

Handel did not mean this entirely as a joke, and he organized his own opera company. For a time, the company seemed to be successful. Soon, however, the inevitable difficulties appeared. A rival company invited an Italian composer, Bononcini, to write for it in the pure Italian style, and not in the German-Italian style, which was ascribed to Handel. A large part of Handel's fickle audiences went over to the other company, especially after a competition in which a neutral composer wrote the first act of an opera, Bononcini the second, and Handel the third. The second act was considered superior to the third, and Bononcini's supporters claimed that this was proof of his general superiority to Handel.

Handel later regained his popularity with several beautiful new operas, and his company once more began to show a profit. However, Handel made another serious error when he hired two famous Italian singers, both female, both temperamental, and both determined to share the spotlight with no one else. One of them enraged Handel so greatly that he is said to have held her by the feet outside a window and threatened to drop her to the ground. This drastic treatment had only a temporary curative effect. The battle between the two singers finally erupted on the stage, in a sensational screaming and hair-pulling match. All London enjoyed the story—except Handel. To him, it meant the failure of his opera.

By this time, Handel had made enemies. He made some because he had firm ideas about how his music should be performed. He made others simply by being a foreigner and not an Englishman. Still others hated him because they hated the king, and the king was his friend. All these reasons for hatred put together spelled failure for Handel's opera company. And as a final blow, along came a sensational and purely English musical satire called *The Beggars' Opera,* whose success was so great that for a time it killed *all* Italian opera in London, that of Bononcini as well as that of Handel.

Handel went so heavily into debt that he became bankrupt. If his father had been alive, he would have had the right to say, "I told you so! Why didn't you become a lawyer?" Handel had often contributed his services to charity, and we can imagine the effect on his pride when in 1738, at the age of fifty-three, he himself was given a benefit concert. Nevertheless, the money raised paid off some of his debts and permitted him to concentrate on music again.

The very next year, he wrote *Israel in Egypt* to the biblical text, an oratorio so beautiful in its vocal and instrumental effects that his audience was left breathless. In 1741 he completed another oratorio, *The Messiah,* first performed in Dublin at a charity concert that Handel himself conducted. The Dublin audience was enthusiastic, and Handel was happier than he had been for years.

The *Hallelujah Chorus* of *The Messiah* is to this day one of the few pieces of music for which all audiences rise to their feet at the first notes and remain standing till the end. The custom is said to have started when the king stood up and the audience had to follow suit.

These oratorios and others that followed brought powerful supporters to Handel, and the fickle audiences turned back to him. Although he did not become wealthy, he did at last have some of the financial security he had so desperately sought. But by this time his health was bad, and he was having trouble with his eyes. One day a coach in which he was riding overturned and Handel was seriously injured. He recovered, but the accident left him weak and tired. In 1752 he underwent an eye operation by the same surgeon who had operated on Bach, and with the same result—total blindness.

He continued to work, dictating his music. But he knew that little time was left him, and in 1759, after several years of suffering, he died. He was buried in Westminster Abbey. Born a German, he was mourned as the greatest British composer.

V

FROM THE BAROQUE
TO THE CLASSICAL

During the lives of Handel, Bach, and Domenico Scarlatti, times
had changed considerably. The changes were most striking in
literature and art. Writers and artists had turned more and more
to nonreligious subjects, and such prominent literary figures as
Voltaire attacked the social abuses that had grown up and flourished under the name of religion, and, in many cases, religion
and the different churches themselves.

The Catholic Church was no longer the only Christian church
in Europe. It had to fight for its life, not only against the individual freethinkers, agnostics, and atheists who assailed it, but also
against the organized opposition of the Lutheran and Anglican
churches, which had split away and fought bitterly for religious
leadership.

The changes in music reflected the changes in other spheres of
life. At the time of Handel's death, the highly ornamented baroque music had already lost part of its audience. Music was becoming increasingly important outside the different churches, and
string instruments such as the violin, viola, and cello were cap-
turing the public taste.

Feudalism, the system under which a nobleman owned the
land, while the peasants tilled it for his benefit, still existed, and
in some countries would continue to exist for another century. But
it was growing perceptibly weaker.

In England and France, brilliant scholars noted what was happening, and wondered what the changes would lead to. Those who were especially sensitive sniffed the revolutions that were still far off.

Meanwhile, for the rich and especially for the nobility, the middle of the eighteenth century was a time of great elegance and sophistication. Fashions in painting, architecture, and furniture acquired a new look—a light, gay, frivolous look. Costume design also changed. Ladies wore prettier, more revealing gowns. Pleasure without regard for cost was the order of the day.

Princes and dukes maintained larger orchestras than ever before and entertained their guests with chamber music and orchestral concerts, as well as with operas.

Composers sought simplicity in instrumental music. The strict rules of counterpoint, so valuable in the composition of religious music dedicated to the exaltation of God, interfered with their expressions of more personal emotions. They now wrote single melodies with accompaniments that would highlight both the melodies and the beauty of tone of the solo instruments. These composers, called "preclassical," helped bridge the gap between the close of the baroque polyphonic period and the classical period of music.

Franz Joseph Haydn (1732–1809)

The first great classical composer was Franz Joseph Haydn, or "Papa" Haydn, as he was affectionately called by the musicians he conducted. The nickname is misleading. It suggests that the music he composed was merely mild and pleasant, and that the conditions under which he worked were always peaceful and serene. It makes us forget that, from early childhood on, Haydn was in a struggle for existence and for the chance to compose at all.

The son of an Austrian wheelwright who lived near the Hungarian border, Haydn began to earn his own living when, at the age of six, he left home. He went to live with a distant cousin, a schoolmaster, who was supposed to teach him music.

It is interesting to note that Franz Joseph was not the only

42. *Franz Joseph Haydn.* (*Courtesy Austrian Information Service*)

member of the Haydn family to become a prominent musician. Michael Haydn (1737–1806), five years younger than Franz Joseph, also became a composer, conductor, and teacher, and for a time Michael's fame overshadowed that of his older brother. By now his compositions have been almost forgotten, but a number of musicians have suggested that they deserve to be revived.

Under the direction of his schoolmaster cousin, young Joseph studied and did whatever chores he was assigned. He was given barely enough to eat, and he was often beaten. But his talent was so great that despite all difficulties, he did become an excellent young musician, able to play the violin and the clavichord.

It was as a boy soprano, however, that he was selected, at the age of eight, to join the children's choir at St. Stephen's Church in Vienna. Here, for almost ten years, he continued to learn music, while enduring the poverty and strict discipline of a choirmaster who treated the choirboys as slaves.

The choir of St. Stephen's played before the Austrian court, and Haydn came to the attention of Empress Maria Theresa herself, but not favorably. She complained that his voice was cracked, probably because it was changing. After that, the choirmaster kept his eye on Haydn more sternly than ever, and when Haydn cut off another choirboy's pigtail, he was discharged at once.

Haydn was then seventeen, and although he had no friends at court, he did have friends among musicians. One of them, Spangler, a tenor who was having a hard time supporting his wife and child, had an attic where he permitted the homeless young man to live. He also helped Haydn to find odd musical jobs, such as playing at weddings and funerals, giving music lessons, copying music, and composing pieces on request.

When he was nineteen years old, Haydn was able to rent a windowless garret on the sixth floor of an apartment house. One of the tenants in the building was Pietro Metastasio, who was highly esteemed as a poet and had written librettos that were used for hundreds of operas. Through him Haydn met Niccolo Porpora (1686–1766), considered the greatest singing teacher who ever lived. Porpora was noted as a miser, and when he found that Haydn was anxious to continue his musical education, he hired the young man as an unpaid personal servant and man-of-all-work, also using Haydn's services as accompanist for the singing lessons he gave.

Porpora's instruction in the composition and performance of music was less helpful than the opportunity Haydn now found to meet wealthy patrons. In 1755 Haydn accepted his first position as director of music for Karl von Furnberg, a wealthy member of the Austrian petty nobility. Haydn held the job for less than a year, but it gave him prestige, and Von Furnberg recommended him to others.

By the time he was twenty-eight, Haydn considered himself finally on the way to fame and fortune, and decided that he could afford to marry. Here he made a serious mistake. His first choice, the daughter of a barber, entered a convent, and Haydn was persuaded to marry her older sister, who was thirty-one. Haydn's married life was unsuccessful from the start, and although he and his wife soon separated, he continued to support her for the rest of her life.

Less than a year after the wedding, Haydn's patron almost went bankrupt and had to dismiss his musicians. By this time Haydn had acquired a reputation as an excellent musician and was quickly hired by Prince Pál Esterhazy, a Hungarian noble-man. When, after less than a year, Prince Pál died, Haydn went with the estate and became assistant chapelmaster to Pál's brother, Prince Nicholas Esterhazy. Five years later, the chapelmaster died, and Haydn was promoted to his place.

For almost twenty-five years more, Haydn remained with the Esterhazy family. Prince Nicholas spent sums equivalent to millions of dollars in creating a palace and grounds that would rival the palace of Louis XV of France at Versailles. But his chief claim to fame in our generation is the work of Haydn. Haydn's duties included composing, conducting, supervision of the musicians, care of the instruments, and care of the music library.

In view of all these duties, the remarkable thing is not only that Haydn composed so much, but that he developed steadily in depth and power as the years rolled on. All his compositions were written to order for the prince, who at first owned them completely, as a master owns the work of his slave. However, Haydn and the prince soon came to an agreement that permitted Haydn to sell some of his compositions to publishers. The increased circulation that Haydn's music attained in this way benefited both his reputation and that of the prince.

Although the prince loved music, and the two men were as friendly as patron and patronized can be, Haydn had to watch his step. The prince played the baryton, a string instrument now obsolete, and Haydn, who had no trouble mastering any instrument, quickly mastered this one in the naïve belief that the prince would be pleased. The prince was in fact far from pleased at the thought of having to compete with a professional, and Haydn

PROSPECT DER FÜRSTLICHEN HAUPT THOR

RESIDENZ ESZTERHAZ VON DEN GEGEN NORDEN.

43. *The Esterhazy Palace, in Hungary, where Haydn lived and worked.* (*Courtesy Austrian Information Service*)

44. *Haydn conducting an operatic performance from the harpsichord (left) in Prince Esterhazy's private theater. (Courtesy Austrian Information Service)*

quickly forgot most of what he knew about playing the baryton. He remembered only enough to compose two hundred pieces for it in such a way that the prince would not find them too difficult to play.

The Esterhazy musicians were well paid, but the estate had no living quarters for their families, and a musician could visit his wife and children only when the prince gave him leave. This did not happen very often, as the prince did not want to disrupt the orchestra's concert schedule. On one occasion, with leaves long overdue, Haydn found a musical way to ask for them. He wrote the parts of a symphony in such a manner that they ended at different times. As soon as his last note was played, each musician blew out his candle, took his instrument, and left.

The prince got the idea, and was so pleased at being told in music what no one would have dared tell him in words, that he gave the musicians their much-needed vacations. The symphony is called the *Farewell Symphony*.

As Haydn's reputation spread, he received commissions and gifts from all over Europe and even from America. Isolated from the rest of the world on the Esterhazy estate, Haydn had no idea how profoundly that world was changing. The aristocracy, to which his own patron belonged, was under attack by writers and playwrights, and in France and other European countries the threat of revolution was in the air.

The new trend in literature and art, known by its German name as *Sturm und Drang*, or *storm and stress*, also showed itself in the music of the younger composers. Haydn had always been willing to learn from other musicians, and now, although internationally acclaimed as the greatest musician alive, he learned from a young man named Mozart how to write music that was more profound and touching than anything he had ever done before. When he met Mozart, Haydn was forty-nine and Mozart only twenty-five. In other musicians, Mozart had encountered jealousy and treachery. In Haydn he was greeted with warm friendship and admiration. Haydn, himself praised as the greatest living composer, insisted that the title belonged to Mozart.

In 1790 Haydn was finally released from his contract by the Esterhazy family and went to England, to which he had been invited long before. His visit was a great success, musically, socially, and even financially. He was received by the queen and given the honorary degree of Doctor of Music by Oxford University.

He returned to Vienna for a time, then went back to England and to more of the honors he had already received. Although the English rulers asked him to remain there, he felt that he was too old to adapt to another language, another way of life, and another climate. He went home to Vienna, worked briefly for the Esterhazy family again, and devoted most of his energy to composition.

Haydn developed the classical form for the structure of the sonata, quartet, and symphony, where themes and movements

45. Haydn at a quartet rehearsal. (Courtesy Austrian Institute in New York)

followed one another in a prescribed manner. He took the best of the musical styles of the time and organized and perfected them into a form that could more readily express the composer's feelings. His music is graceful, humorous, at times powerful, and always imbued with a folk music character. Haydn came from a peasant background, and he used the folk tunes of his native Austria and of his Hungarian neighbors. But he altered these tunes according to the needs of his sonatas and symphonies, and he created a tremendous number of melodies that sounded like folk tunes but were in fact his own.

Despite the limitations of the orchestra of his time, he changed the manner in which the different instruments were used. The name "classical" is used for this style of music because it became the classic model for the symphonic form. The music of Mozart is also considered classical, and so is the music of their contemporaries. Composers of later periods who used this symphonic form are called *"neoclassic,"* or "new" or "modified" classicists. Haydn had no suspicion that his music was classical. No one told him.

In 1805 the rumor spread through Europe that Haydn had died. A special memorial concert was arranged in Paris to honor his memory, only to be canceled when it was learned that he was alive. Haydn regretted the cancellation; he would have liked to conduct the concert himself.

Fortunately, during his last years Haydn received many honors and tributes from the public and from the most distinguished musicians of his day without having to die first.

The French had been anxious to honor him in Paris. Now they paid their respects in Vienna. When their armies, under Napoleon, invaded Austria and bombarded the pleasure-loving city, Haydn, who was fiercely patriotic, called his household staff together to sing the Austrian national anthem, which he had written. The French did not hold this against him. When Vienna was occupied, Napoleon placed an honor guard around Haydn's home to protect him from vandals. The guard could not protect him from death, however, which came to Haydn on May 31, 1809.

Wolfgang Amadeus Mozart (1756–91)

Wolfgang Amadeus Mozart was born with the greatest natural gifts granted to any individual in the history of music. In early childhood he had skilled hands, an unbelievably keen ear, a nearly perfect musical memory, and a wonderful musical imagination. At the age of six he could talk with most professional musicians as their equal.

Born in Salzburg, Austria, he was the son of a well-known

46. *The six-year-old Mozart at the court of Queen Maria Theresa, whose arm enfolds her daughter, Marie Antoinette. (Courtesy Austrian Information Service)*

musician, Leopold Mozart (1719–87). Wolfgang learned to play the clavichord by listening to his older sister practice and then imitating her, although he did take formal lessons later. In a similar way, he learned to play the violin by watching and listening to the professional violinists who visited their home.

Leopold Mozart was a member of the orchestra of the Archbishop of Salzburg and was newly appointed to the position of court composer. As Wolfgang's genius became apparent, however, Leopold took leave from his work and set about exploiting the talents of his children. Wolfgang was then six and his sister, Nannerl, eleven. Both children were fine musicians, but Wolfgang's lesser age made him the main attraction to the audiences.

Leopold first took them to Munich, where they had a tremendous success, and then to Vienna, where their success was even greater. In addition to playing at sight difficult music for the clavichord and violin, Wolfgang played the clavichord with his hands under a cloth that covered the keyboard, and improvised on different keyboard instruments.

The Empress of Austria led her court in idolizing the children, and both Wolfgang and his sister received court costumes and gifts of money. At the height of this early triumph, however, Wolfgang was stricken with scarlet fever. After he recovered, he was taken back to Salzburg. This first tour of his, lasting less than a year, had been successful in many ways, but expenses had been high, and by the time Leopold and his children reached home again, they found themselves, financially, about where they had started.

The next tour lasted three and a half years and included triumphant concerts in Paris, London, and The Hague before the crowned heads of France, England, and the Netherlands. On the way from one capital city to another, the two children also gave countless performances before less distinguished audiences in small towns.

Money and gifts, if not showered, were at least sprinkled upon the touring Mozarts. But the entire family was in bad health. Travel in creaky horse-drawn carriages over bad roads in all kinds of weather and the strain of being always on exhibition affected both Leopold and the children. Wolfgang and his sister were under additional strain—that of having to keep adult hours because of the need to play for adults.

Part of the tour was exciting and enjoyable, including a vacation in Switzerland. But by the time the Mozart family returned to Salzburg, most of the money the children had earned had once more gone to pay for the expenses of travel and medical treatment.

Back home again, Leopold realized that Nannerl, at sixteen, could no longer pass as a child prodigy, while Wolfgang, at eleven, was approaching the end of his own career in that line, and would soon be in open competition with adults. Leopold knew that for a musician, whether genius or not, nothing was as comforting as a steady income, and he now began to look around for a position of this kind for Wolfgang.

47. Mozart at seven accompanies his father, Leopold, and his sister, Nannerl.
(*Courtesy Austrian Information Service*)

The Archbishop of Salzburg, his own employer, seemed like a good patron for Wolfgang, but the archbishop was not a trusting soul, and the reports of Wolfgang's musical abilities did not allay his suspicions. Perhaps, he thought, Leopold was composing music which he then palmed off as Wolfgang's.

He therefore had Wolfgang locked into a room of his palace, and ordered him to write music for part of an oratorio, the rest of which would be composed by two other musicians. Not until the boy had completed the music was he allowed to go free.

Hoping to cash in on the reputation that Wolfgang had made on his first trip to Vienna, Leopold Mozart took his son and daughter to that city once more. But the trip was a disaster. Wolfgang and his sister were both stricken with smallpox and were slow to recover. Wolfgang himself was blind for nine days.

When Wolfgang finally saw the empress again, he was rewarded for his playing with a medal but no money. The empress had appointed her son, Josef, to rule Austria as emperor with her, and the new emperor complained that he was poor and had to cut down on expenses. Some of the nobility followed their emperor's example, and many musicians found themselves suddenly unemployed.

The emperor did commission Wolfgang to write an opera, and the boy quickly completed *La Finta semplice* (*The Pretended Simpleton*), but the jealousy of other composers prevented it from being performed.

The Mozarts returned to Salzburg, where the archbishop appointed Wolfgang concertmaster of his orchestra. The title was honorary, and there was no salary. Leopold was disappointed, but he still had other plans. The next year, when Wolfgang was thirteen, father and son set off for Italy.

Here Wolfgang was more successful than ever. His concerts were sold out, and an opera he wrote, *Mitridate, rè di Ponto* (*Mithridates, King of Pontus*), was a great hit.

One incident in his Italian tour was enough in itself to make him famous. Wolfgang had visited the Sistine Chapel in order to hear the *Miserere*, the setting of a psalm by the composer Allegri.

48. Mozart and his sister play a duet for their father. The portrait on the wall is of their dead mother. (Courtesy Austrian Information Service)

The music, which was extremely complicated, belonged to the pope, and no copies were permitted to be made, on pain of excommunication. After one hearing, Mozart wrote out the entire composition from memory, returning for a second hearing to correct a few notes of which he was uncertain. The pope heard of this almost incredible feat and, instead of excommunicating Mozart, made him a papal knight.

From now on, as Mozart became an adult, his life became a seemingly endless round of musical success and financial failure. He returned to Salzburg, where the old archbishop had died, and a new one had been appointed. To go with his title of concertmaster, Mozart received a salary of a hundred and fifty gulden—about seventy-five dollars a year, for which he was expected to compose tremendous amounts of music, including operas.

The new archbishop was a miserable character under whose rule life was a torture. When Mozart tendered his resignation, the archbishop had him literally kicked out of the house.

Escaping temporarily from the archbishop, Mozart tried Italy again, then Vienna, and once more Munich. Nowhere was he offered the secure position he sought. His second visit to Paris was particularly painful, first because his mother died and was buried there, and then because it was impressed upon him that many of the French aristocrats regarded a musician as a rather low form of servant. One example will suffice. Mozart had been asked to play for the Duchess de Chabot, and on arriving at the duchess's home was kept waiting in an icy room for a half hour. When he was finally commanded to play, he asked for permission to warm his hands at a fire for a few minutes and was refused. He had to play immediately, on an out-of-tune piano, while the duchess and her friends chatted without paying attention to him. No wonder Mozart frequently expressed his contempt for the aristocracy.

Even Haydn, one of the few musicians who did not envy Mozart, was unable to help him obtain a good position. Perhaps some of the fault was Mozart's own, although much of it was due to the time in which he lived. Europe was full of composers, and each one needed a patron. Mozart did not know how to connive against other musicians, and he had not mastered the art of stabbing a friend in the back. He had, at least for a time, the naïve idea that the quality of his music alone would help him to succeed.

Mozart had met people from the highest to the lowest rungs of the social ladder and, as his operas show, had an insight into their feelings and behavior. Yet in his personal life he was frequently the victim of intrigues by other musicians. During his final illness, Mozart suspected that he had been poisoned by a jealous rival, Antonio Salieri (1750–1825). There is no doubt that Salieri poisoned his life by slandering him, turning patrons and critics against him, and doing whatever other mischief his petty mind could think of. But there is also no evidence that he poisoned Mozart in any legal sense.

The way in which Mozart allowed himself to be married also indicates how naïve he was. At the age of twenty-one he met the Weber family, musicians whose fame would reach the heights in their relative, the composer Carl Maria von Weber. The Webers that Mozart knew were a cold-blooded lot, although it took him some time to realize this. He fell in love with one of them, Aloysia, a singer, and spent much of his time teaching her and writing vocal music for her. When she felt that she had used him enough for her purposes, she married someone else, and the Webers shrewdly convinced Mozart that their second daughter, Constanze, was the wife he needed. He married Constanze, unhappily, in 1782.

The portraits of Mozart as a child show the face of a charming, alert, and even mischievous boy. Those of his later life touch us by the look of hopeless sadness in his eyes. Much of his suffering was due to the vindictiveness of other musicians and the thoughtless cruelty of patrons. Some of it, however, was the result of his marriage.

For Constanze was almost exactly the kind of wife Mozart did not need. Mozart was highly industrious and turned out string quartets, quintets, symphonies, concertos, songs, and operas, to support his growing family. He was not paid well, but at least he was often paid. Unfortunately, he was too careless with his money, spending it recklessly or lending to others when he had it and borrowing when it was scarce. In this respect, Constanze was much like him, only worse. She was flighty, self-centered, and her spending was more often for herself than for others.

Partly because of his marriage to Constanze, Mozart became estranged from his father. Although they made up later, they never again became as close as they had been before Wolfgang's marriage.

At the performance of *Die Entführung aus dem Serail* (*The Elopement from the Harem*), Emperor Josef complained that the opera contained too many notes. "Just as many notes as are needed," replied Mozart, "no more, no less." Many years after Mozart's death, it became fashionable for critics to complain that

49. *Mozart toward the end of his life. From an unfinished portrait by J. Lange. (Courtesy Austrian Information Service)*

as a composer he was childlike and that his music was all surface prettiness, with no depth. Mozart's music was much more profound than many of his listeners realized. It is true that because of his need for money, Mozart wrote many potboilers, compositions that he himself knew to be inferior. But as he himself said, "He who judges me by my worst works is a scoundrel." And it should be added that even some of the compositions that he scrawled hastily to earn a few gulden were masterpieces.

The operas he wrote in his teens do not equal the magical works he wrote as a mature composer, but they do contain many delightful passages. His later operas are among the greatest in the world. *The Marriage of Figaro,* first given in Prague, was such a tremendous success that its tunes were sung and played in all sorts of arrangements. In a following opera, *Don Giovanni,* Mozart alludes playfully to the popularity of Figaro when he has a small orchestra on stage play a few bars of the earlier opera, and he has Don Giovanni sing, "I'm tired of that tune, I've heard it too often."

Also given its first performance at Prague, *Don Giovanni* was an even more sensational success than *The Marriage of Figaro.* Given in Vienna later on, it was received coldly. It is now considered among the finest operas ever written; some poeple consider it to be unsurpassed.

Toward the end of 1787, Gluck died, and Mozart was appointed in his place as chamber composer to the Emperor Josef. But where Gluck had received two thousand gulden a year, Mozart received only eight hundred. It was too little and far too late. Mozart had only four more years to live.

These four years of pain and misery saw the composition of some of his most beautiful music, including three of the most magnificent symphonies ever written and another operatic masterpiece, *The Magic Flute,* which Mozart completed shortly before his death. *The Magic Flute* was written to a confused plot concocted by Emanuel Schikaneder, a producer and brother Mason.

The Masonic order, to which both Haydn and Mozart belonged, was a society that supported the liberal ideas of that time and emphasized the equality and brotherhood of man. In the United States (or the American Colonies, before the American Revolution) it included such men as Benjamin Franklin and George Washington. The plot of *The Magic Flute* makes little sense and the opera is full of what has been called Masonic symbolism. But to most operagoers, Mozart's music more than makes up for the weaknesses of the plot. Beethoven considered it Mozart's greatest opera.

In July 1791, a mysterious man dressed in gray appeared in Mozart's house and asked him to write a Requiem, for which he would receive a very large sum, on condition that he never try to learn the name of his patron. The visitor left a number of gulden as a retainer. Mozart kept putting off the work, on the ground that he was busy with other things, and especially because he had a morbid feeling that the Requiem would be sung at his own funeral. But the mysterious stranger, whom Mozart regarded as the messenger of death, made another appearance, and Mozart, now bedridden, finally set to work.

He died with the *Requiem* still unfinished. He never learned that the messenger came not from Death, but from a Count von Walsegg, who wanted to be considered a musician and would order compositions from professional composers and pass them off as his own. After Mozart's death, he tried to do this with the *Requiem,* which was completed by Franz Xaver Süssmayr, a pupil of Mozart. Constanze, however, arranged for publication in Mozart's name and foiled the count.

Mozart's bad luck followed him even after death. The day of his funeral was so stormy that the mourners never reached the cemetery where he was to be buried, and his coffin was thrown into a common grave, in a place now unknown.

VI

FROM CLASSICAL MUSIC
TO THE DAWN OF THE ROMANTIC

At the end of the eighteenth century and the beginning of the nineteenth, tremendous changes were taking place in almost every aspect of American and European life. The revolution that freed the American colonies from Great Britain profoundly affected both countries and set an example that later helped bring about the French Revolution and the wars that swept across Europe from France to Russia.

The Industrial Revolution, which began in England about 1760, introduced more and more machines to perform the work previously done by skilled craftsmen. Thousands of men, women, and children were hired to work in factories that used the new methods, while thousands of others, like the weavers who wove cotton at home, were thrown out of work.

The use of machines increased the production of such important commodities as cloth and iron products, and eventually brought about a higher standard of living. But the years during which the rapid change took place were painful for many people, including artists. The old system, in which artists worked for a noble patron, still existed in such countries as Italy and Austria for a time. But the king and the aristocrats who had been the patrons of art in France were either killed or driven from the country. The new patrons who took their place were either wealthy businessmen or the general public.

Painters, writers, and composers also responded to the changing world about them through their art. Trained in techniques inherited from the past, most of them, nevertheless, began to experiment with new methods of expressing themselves. These artists were the bridge to the romantic period. Their leader was a musical giant whose mind and heart anticipated the future.

Ludwig van Beethoven (1770–1827)

Ludwig van Beethoven, one of the giants of music, never heard his most famous works performed. Afflicted from the age of twenty-six with deafness that became worse from year to year, he was gradually shut out from the world around him. During the last few years of his embittered life, while thousands of people enjoyed his music, he himself could hear only the sounds that his own mind created within him.

As a child in the German city of Bonn, Beethoven could look back on his father's side at two generations of musicians—and alcoholics. Both his father and his father's father had been minor court musicians. Either disappointment in their careers drove them to drink or drink made it impossible for them to have successful careers.

Ludwig's mother, a kind and gentle woman who was browbeaten by her almost continually drunken husband, did all she could to protect her children from their father. The elder Beethoven started Ludwig's musical training at the age of four, and although the child showed talent, young Ludwig was not the prodigy that Mozart had been. His father, however, thought that this was a mere matter of practice.

Ludwig became a child without a childhood. His life consisted of endless hours at the piano, violin, and viola, with occasional beatings for not practicing enough or for making mistakes.

Ludwig gave his first concert at the age of eight, and another at the age of eleven. Neither of these concerts was a great success. However, his playing aroused the interest of Christian Gottlob Neefe, the court organist of Cologne. Neefe taught Beethoven

50. *Ludwig van Beethoven as a young man.* (*Courtesy Austrian Information Service*)

music and developed his interest in other arts. Beethoven was always grateful to Neefe, and in later life, when Beethoven wrote a letter acknowledging his debt to the older man, Neefe proudly published it.

Thanks to Neefe's help, Beethoven became assistant court organist to the Elector of Cologne, and at the age of thirteen was earning a hundred and fifty florins a year—half his father's salary. He was also learning a great deal about composition and about the art of conducting an orchestra.

When he was sixteen he made a trip to Vienna and played for Mozart, who was greatly impressed by his talent. But he returned home to nurse his mother through the last stages of tuberculosis. When she died, he found himself head of the family, for his father, now always drunk, was in and out of jail. Ludwig himself suffered from asthma, and the illness was made worse by the heavy load of responsibility placed upon him.

By now his talent had impressed many musicians and made him some good friends. In 1792, when Haydn passed through Bonn on his way back from London, he heard Beethoven play and offered to teach him in Vienna.

Beethoven left for Vienna again a month or so before his twenty-third birthday. His patron, the Elector of Cologne, was not far behind him, for the French Revolution was at its height and French troops occupied Bonn shortly after the elector left.

Although Haydn kept his promise to give him lessons and charged very little, Beethoven was dissatisfied. He felt that Haydn was giving him too little attention, and it soon became clear that they had different attitudes to music, as well as to the world in which they lived. Without telling Haydn, Beethoven began to take lessons from another teacher.

Beethoven would not tolerate the old relationship that had existed between musician and patron. The musician had been a servant and had been treated as one. Sometimes he was treated well, as Haydn himself had been treated by the Esterhazy family, sometimes very badly, as Mozart had been treated by the Archbishop of Salzburg. The musician's happiness and life depended on the whim of his patron. And although Mozart, for example, rebelled against this semislavery, and expressed some of his own feelings about equality in *The Marriage of Figaro,* the time of the musician's liberation did not arrive until Mozart was at the point of death. Liberation came with the French Revolution, which started in 1789.

In the years that followed, Beethoven never again entered the service of a nobleman. He supported himself at first as a concert pianist and wrote many of his piano works for himself as performer. He was a magnificent pianist, and his listeners often expressed regret that he had abandoned the concert stage to concentrate on composition.

Among the great men whose friendship Beethoven enjoyed was Goethe, famous as a poet, dramatist, novelist, and even as a man of science. Goethe heard some of Beethoven's symphonies, especially the third and the fifth, and shuddered. He could not deny Beethoven's genius, but the Beethoven symphonies shook him out of his compromise with life, and he did not want to hear them again.

Beethoven's ideas about freedom and the brotherhood and equality of men were expressed not only in his music but in his daily behavior. He would not sit at the servants' table in the house of a prince. If a countess begged him to play and he did not feel like it, he would not play. In an age when no man at court was considered decently dressed without a powdered wig, he wore his own unkempt mop of hair. He was impatient, irritable, sometimes boorish. But he was never cruel, in the arrogant, unthinking manner of the lofty aristocrat.

The differences in attitude between him and Goethe are strikingly revealed in a story that Beethoven himself told. He and Goethe had been out walking, when they noticed the Empress of Austria and her retinue coming toward them. Beethoven linked Goethe's arm in his, and said, "They must make way for us, not we for them." Goethe, who had himself acquired the manners of a courtier, freed his arm, moved aside, removed his hat, and bowed low as the imperial group approached. Beethoven, however, con-

51. Contemporary sketches of Beethoven and examples of his signature. (Courtesy Metropolitan Museum of Art, Crosby Brown Collection, 1901)

tinued to walk ahead, merely tipping his hat to the group, which respectfully made way for him.

Beethoven fell in love several times but never married. He was usually attracted to women of culture, most of whom seemed to enjoy having a genius as a friend, without wanting to have him as a husband. We know that he wrote a tortured letter to a woman he called "Immortal Beloved." Students of music history have been racking their brains for a century and a half, trying to decide who she was, and why Beethoven did not marry her. Perhaps it was because he knew that he would be a difficult man to live with or that his work would suffer if he had to consider the rights and feelings of a wife.

From the time he first realized that he was becoming deaf, his life was more painful than ever. He even thought of committing suicide, as he wrote in a letter to his two brothers, the so-called "Heiligenstadt Testament." Here he told of the despair that had overwhelmed him for the six years after the first symptoms appeared, and of the false hopes through which he had been cheated by the physicians who treated him. As a man whose entire career depended on the keenness of his hearing, he could not let even his friends suspect that he was becoming deaf. In conversation, he pretended to understand remarks he could not hear, and before his deafness became known, many people must have suspected, from the inappropriate answers he gave, that he was going out of his mind.

After his father died, Beethoven was for a time free of family troubles. His brothers supported themselves. In fact, his brother Johann became very well to do and apparently wanted to forget that he was the son of an unsuccessful musician and a cook, for on one occasion, when he signed his name to a document in Ludwig's presence, he added "Landowner." Ludwig at once signed his own name, and added "Brainowner."

Beethoven was on better terms with his other brother, Karl. Karl made an unsuccessful marriage, from which he escaped by dying. Ludwig adopted his dead brother's son, also named Karl, but he had to carry on a long legal battle with the boy's mother, and he had many difficulties with the boy himself. Beethoven's nephew, suffering first from neglect and then from too much attention, grew up to be completely self-centered and regarded his famous uncle as a sentimental fool from whom he could obtain money whenever he needed it.

Beethoven himself had little money to spare. In order to keep him in Vienna, several members of the nobility had promised him a steady income, but for various reasons some of the money was delayed or not paid at all.

With all the problems that Beethoven faced—in regard to money, relatives, bad health, and, above all, the curse of his ever-increasing deafness—he continued to compose. He could compose,

52. *The mature Beethoven.* (*Courtesy Austrian Information Service*)

53. *Beethoven's study. (Courtesy Austrian Information Service)*

if need be, with great speed, and his ability to improvise at the piano was in itself enough to make him famous. But Beethoven's standards were higher than those of his listeners. His notebooks show how he would return time and again to some simple little melody, change the notes, modify the rhythm, and eventually produce one of the striking themes that are part of his famous symphonies.

Beethoven's symphonies followed the classical pattern of the Haydn symphonies, but they were longer and more complex. Beethoven wrote for a larger orchestra, and he used his instruments with more independence than had Haydn or Mozart. Beethoven's genius was thus able to express itself more fully. His orchestration served as the inspiration and model for all the composers who followed him.

His compositions express the powerful feelings of their creator: his love of nature and of life, despite his tormented unhappiness; his robust and mischievous humor; his heroic imagination; his sublime faith in a joyful and just world in the future. The lasting popularity of his works is testimony that his listeners also share his emotions, if not his vision.

Beethoven wrote nine symphonies, an opera, *Fidelio*, five piano concertos, a violin concerto, many quartets, trios, and other chamber works, thirty-two piano sonatas, ten violin sonatas, ten cello sonatas, as well as other works for solo instrument, voice, or orchestra.

In his composition, Beethoven could usually shut out for a time all nonmusical thoughts. Yet there were occasions when even this failed him, and he would rush out, completely distracted, unaware of how he was dressed, and walk through the countryside in the hope of finding inner peace. On one such occasion he was arrested as a tramp but was quickly released as soon as he was identified.

Isolated as he seemed, Beethoven knew what was going on in the world of his time. He hailed the French Revolution and originally dedicated to Napoleon Bonaparte his third symphony, the one that he himself considered his greatest. But when Napoleon had himself crowned emperor and embarked on foreign conquest, Beethoven angrily tore up the old dedication and wrote a new one: "To the memory of a great man."

Beethoven's stature as a composer was so great that he was free of petty jealousy. He hailed such young newcomers as Franz Schubert, Carl Maria von Weber, Gioacchino Rossini, and Luigi Cherubini.

Beethoven suffered through a number of treatments for dropsy and, during the latter part of his life, grew worse from one month to the next. He died in 1827 during a thunderstorm, a fitting symbol for his stormy life. Just as he was dying, the news spread that Beethoven had been sent a large sum of money from England to make his life easier. The thrifty Viennese did not let the money go to waste. For the previously planned second-class funeral they now substituted a first-class one. Twenty thousand people lined the streets to pay their last respects, and in the funeral procession itself were outstanding musicians and writers of the day. In the short interval from Mozart to Beethoven, composers had made great progress—at least as far as funerals were concerned.

Carl Maria von Weber (1786–1826)

Mozart had a great deal to answer for. The example he set, by touring as a child prodigy, led hundreds of parents to search for child prodigies in their own families. All over Europe, children sat before pianos and practiced grimly for careers in music that in most cases never developed.

Beethoven was one of the exceptions who eventually made good. Carl Maria von Weber was another. In Weber's case, parental pressure was intense, for Mozart had married into the family, and young Weber was a cousin of Mozart's wife, Constanze. Weber's parents must have had disagreements on many subjects, for his father was fifty-one and his mother eighteen when Carl was born, but from the moment that the child showed talent—and this was almost as soon as he was out of the cradle—both agreed that their son would be a child prodigy.

Weber's father had been a soldier and a district judge, among other things. Now he was the impresario or manager of a touring opera company, and he arranged to have his young son play for audiences. The life of a touring company was a difficult one, and Carl, who had been born with a hip disease that lamed him for life, seems to have suffered in health still further. But constant exposure to the operatic environment taught him a great deal. Later he studied with a fashionable teacher, Abbé Vogler, and showed such exceptional talent that the abbé was able to have him appointed conductor of the opera in Breslau when he was just seventeen years old.

As in Mozart's case, success created enemies. Other contenders for the post were bitterly disappointed, as well as ashamed to lose

54. The youthful Carl Maria von Weber. (Courtesy German Information Center)

to a seventeen-year-old. The musicians in the orchestra resented taking orders from him, especially when he proved to be very strict and demanding. Weber remained conductor for two not very happy years, but outside working hours he made a number of friends with whom he led a dissolute life. A good part of his time was spent in drinking and chasing after the young women of Breslau.

Weber gave up his position as conductor to take a much more enjoyable one as musical director for Duke Eugen of Württemberg, a small German kingdom. This position lasted less than a year, coming to an end at the approach of the French armies. The Duke Eugen went off to lead his troops against Napoleon, leaving Weber behind as a sort of secretary to his younger brother, Duke Ludwig. Weber's duties consisted of keeping track of Ludwig's confused financial affairs and trying to secure from the oldest brother, King Friedrich, enough money to pay Ludwig's debts and Weber's salary.

The nature of his work did not endear Weber to King Friedrich, who hated to part with money. It was one of Weber's practical jokes, however, that made the king his complete enemy. One day an old woman asked Weber where the royal washerwoman was, and he pointed out the king's room. The king's reaction can easily be imagined, and Weber was lucky that the king did not immediately roar, "Off with his head!" Weber was jailed, however, until Duke Ludwig managed to set him free.

But the king remained hostile and merely waited for another opportunity to strike. He found it in Weber's family life. Weber's mother had died ten years before, and his father, now over seventy, was living with him. The old man had a shady history, and an investigation by the king's agents turned up evidence of dishonest financial dealing. The king was also irritated by the old man's pretensions. The *von* in his name, an indication of nobility, had been assumed without right, and, to make matters worse, he had taken to calling himself Baron.

The king took great satisfaction in banishing both Carl and his father from Württemberg. The young man was for a time dazed by the blow. An opera of his was in rehearsal, and he was also in love with one of the singers. Now both opera and love affair were finished. The important thing was to make a living for his father and himself.

Somehow Carl managed. He went on tours as a concert pianist, he composed operas and other works, he recalled himself to the attention of Abbé Vogler, and he made friends who respected his ability and were able to help him. One of his friends was Giacomo Meyerbeer (1791–1864), five years younger than Weber himself, and in his twenties already a great success as an operatic composer.

In 1813, Weber had the luck to be in Prague at a time when a director of the opera there was badly needed. He secured the appointment at an unexpectedly high salary, and at once set to work, hiring new singers, improving the quality of the orchestra, and watching over all the details of scenery and costumes. By this time he had strong German nationalist feelings, and he became bitter about the Prague audiences and their preference for the Italian operas of Rossini. Apparently he did not realize that the Prague audiences, who were mainly Czechs, would have no special love for operas that glorified their German rulers.

In the German states themselves, nationalist feelings were on the rise, and Weber became famous all over Germany by writing music to a group of patriotic songs, and then following this with a patriotic cantata.

He left Prague late in 1816, and a few months later was appointed by the King of Saxony director of the opera house in Dresden. Here he married happily, and he composed *Der Freischütz* (*The Marksman*) based on a German folk tale. This opera was given its first performance in Berlin in June of 1821, and was so sensationally successful, not only in Berlin, but all over Germany, that it put an end to the dominance of Italian opera in Germany.

In 1825 Weber knew that he was dying of tuberculosis. Nonetheless he undertook a trip to London for the first performance of his *Oberon*, written to make sure that his wife and children would not

55. *Carl Maria von Weber, frail and ill.* (*Courtesy German Information Center*)

be left penniless. On the way to England he stopped off in Paris, where he met Rossini and apologized for the unfairness of some of his criticism. Rossini received him warmly, and the two men parted on good terms.

In London the performance of *Oberon*, whose original libretto was in English, was a tremendous success. The piano concerts that Weber gave were less successful, especially one that conflicted with a horse race. Death came to him while he was still in London, in his fortieth year.

Weber was a pioneer of the romantic movement. In his use of the orchestra, his dedication to the development of German opera, and his interest in folk legends, he led the way that many later composers followed.

Gioacchino Antonio Rossini (*1792–1868*)

Gioacchino Rossini was born in the small town of Pesaro, where his father was inspector of slaughterhouses as well as town trumpeter. His mother was a singer and with her husband toured from one small theater to another, while Gioacchino was left at home with relatives. Although his father did not apparently try to train him in either of his own skills, he did, for a short time, apprentice the boy to a blacksmith. Young Rossini was an obedient son, but he soon decided that shoeing horses was not for him.

When the family moved to Bologna, a fairly large city, Rossini studied music, mastered several instruments, and became a boy soprano. He never completed his musical studies, but by the time he was eighteen he had enough skill, enough experience, and enough self-confidence to consider himself a composer.

His idol was Mozart, and he tried so hard to be like Mozart that he was nicknamed "The Little German." His first opera, in one act, was a great success in Venice. From then on there could be no doubt: he *was* a composer, and on the way to being an extremely successful one. Music flowed from his pen whenever it was needed —not very profound, but pleasant, enjoyable, and of a kind that appealed to his audiences.

At twenty-one, he now experienced the kind of disaster that at one time or another befalls every one in the theater. Music continued to flow from his pen—but opera after opera failed. Nursing his injured feelings, Rossini went back to Bologna to recover.

In Bologna, he had an unexpected visit from the impresario of opera at Naples, who offered him the position of musical director of two opera houses. Rossini would receive a good salary as well as a percentage of the profits from the gambling tables that the impresario operated.

By this time Rossini had recovered his self-confidence. He wrote an opera that was a triumph, not only because of his music, but because of the acting of a Spanish soprano, Isabella Colbran. Seven

56. *Rossini, plump and prosperous, thanks to his talents.* (*Courtesy French Embassy Press and Information Division*)

57. *A scene from an early production of* The Barber of Seville. *Photo by Pic.* (*Courtesy Paris Opera Museum*)

years older than Rossini, Colbran was a beautiful woman, and Rossini wrote his opera in a way that displayed all her best qualities as a singer and actress. Then he took a leave of absence to write two operas for production in Rome.

His first Roman offering was a rank failure and was jeered by the audience. But he still had his contract for a second opera, and in less than two weeks he wrote all the music, although he did speed things up a bit by borrowing from some of his earlier operas. The new opera was *The Barber of Seville*. Like Mozart's *The Marriage of Figaro*, it was based on a play by Beaumarchais, and it dealt with the earlier story of some of the same characters that Mozart had put on the stage.

The music was lively and sparkling. It still sparkles today. But at its first performance in February 1816 the opera was a dismal failure. Rossini had made the mistake of using a story that had already served for the libretto of an extremely popular opera by Giovanni Paisiello, and the first-night audience would have none of it.

This time Rossini did not retreat to Bologna. The next night the *Barber* was performed again. This time it was better received, and within a few weeks it was a hit. Within a few seasons it became the most popular opera in all Europe.

Immensely pleased with himself, Rossini returned to Naples, where he continued to write operas. In 1820, however, a revolution overthrew the king, and two years later Rossini and Isabella Colbran left Naples. They were married on the way to Vienna, where they were greeted with acclaim.

From Vienna, Rossini returned to Venice and then, after several months, journeyed to London, where he was honored by King George IV as well as by the public.

Only Paris, at this time the opera capital of the world, remained to be conquered, and it was to Paris that Rossini and his wife went. There were malicious rumors that Rossini had married Isabella for her money, and the accusation might have been true, for at the time of their marriage Rossini, although a successful composer, was not yet a wealthy one. Impresarios in half a dozen countries pirated his operas and paid him no royalties. In contrast, a singer could receive a fantastic sum for a single performance, and there were then no recording devices to pirate her singing and acting.

At any rate, for some years Rossini was a devoted husband, even after his success in Paris made him independent of his wife's money. He succeeded in getting the French king, Charles X, to sign a contract awarding him a pension of six thousand francs a year for life. Then he wrote *William Tell*, which was produced in 1829, and he stopped writing operas.

He was then only thirty-seven, and he had thirty-nine years yet to live. Perhaps he was unhappy about the reception of *William Tell*, which the critics liked and the public did not. Perhaps he was lazy, and perhaps he felt that he was past his prime as a com-

58. Rossini in retirement. (New York Public Library)

poser. Whatever the reason, he composed opera no more. During the rest of his life, only two religious works and a few smaller compositions came from his once prolific pen.

After years of separation, Isabella died and Rossini married again. When he and his second wife finally settled down in Paris after years of wandering, their apartment became the center of attraction for the writers, painters, and musicians of Europe. Among the musicians who came to pay their respects were Richard Wagner, Franz Liszt, and Giuseppe Verdi. Rossini, who in his earlier years had been a master of intrigue, could be very warm-hearted and generous to those who did not attack him. During his years of retirement he became noted as an excellent amateur chef, and a dinner invitation from Rossini was eagerly sought after.

Rossini's music, especially that of his comic operas, has survived surprisingly well. Audiences still chuckle over *The Barber of Seville, Cinderella,* and *The Italian in Algiers. William Tell,* a serious romantic opera, was a failure at its first performance, but became extremely popular. The ballet music and other orchestral excerpts are frequently heard.

Franz Peter Schubert (*1797–1828*)

Like Purcell, Haydn, and Rossini, Franz Schubert took a great step forward in his professional career by becoming a choirboy. Schubert learned, during his career as a boy soprano, almost as much about music as he was to learn during the rest of his life.

Schubert was the twelfth of fourteen children born in Lichtenthal, a suburb of Vienna, to a schoolmaster, Franz Schubert, and his wife. Young Franz was one of the few Schuberts who survived the diseases of infancy and childhood.

A schoolmaster's salary was not a large one, but it was enough to keep the Schubert family from starving, and Franz had a happy childhood. In those days a schoolmaster had to teach music as well as reading, writing, and arithmetic, and all the Schuberts

59. *Franz Schubert.* (*Courtesy Austrian Information Service*)

were taught to play one instrument or another. Franz Schubert's mother was related to several professional musicians, but there was no musician on either his father's or his mother's side who had anything like the talent of young Franz.

When Franz was eleven, he passed an audition for chorister in a school named the Imperial Convict. *Convict* meant a community and was not intended to suggest that the boys who worked in it were prisoners, although in fact they sometimes were treated as such. The school was attached to the University of Vienna, and in it the choristers lived and studied. Franz stayed until he was sixteen, acquiring some knowledge of other subjects in addition to music.

The happiness of Schubert's childhood appears to have ended when he entered the school. Apart from the chance it gave him to learn music, he disliked it intensely. He was usually cold in winter, and always hungry no matter what the season. The school authorities did not believe in pampering their students by heating their rooms or feeding them well.

The elder Franz Schubert found music enjoyable, but not profitable, and he hoped that his son would become a schoolmaster like himself, a respected member of the community with a regular income. Young Franz, however, had no idea of spending his life teaching subjects he hated. He liked to sing, to play, and to conduct the school orchestra, and above all he loved to compose. Soon the father realized that his good-for-nothing son, as he now began to think of Franz, was spending more time composing music than studying his school subjects. Father and son argued violently, and young Schubert was told either to forget about being a composer or to forget about ever coming home again.

Schubert chose to remain a composer. He studied for a very short time with Antonio Salieri, the former rival of Mozart, now director of the training school. But he had little interest in Salieri's theory of composition and soon stopped taking lessons from him.

The death of Schubert's mother brought him and his father together again, and as a result he did actually become his father's assistant in teaching school. His forebodings were correct: he hated the work. He was happy only in his free time, when he could compose. Nevertheless, he endured it for three years, as he had fallen in love, and hoped to get a better position that would enable him to marry. But he did not get the position, and under pressure from her family, his fiancée eventually married a man who had a good income.

Young Franz gave up teaching for good, to lead the kind of life that later became known as bohemian, and still later as beatnik. He had no steady income, no regular meals, and no home, except for the lodgings his friends could find for him. His friends, some of whom he had known from his early days at the Convict, like him, enjoyed sitting in the gay Viennese cafés, drinking wine and beer and going to parties, theaters, and operas.

At seventeen, Schubert composed the love song *Gretchen am Spinnrade* (*Gretchen at the Spinning Wheel*), and at eighteen the spine-tingling and tragic *Der Erlkönig* (*The Erl King*). *The Erl King*, recognized as one of the masterpieces of vocal literature, was rejected by several publishers and waited six years for its first public performance.

Unlike Beethoven, whom he revered, Schubert did not spend days or years of agonizing thought trying to find the best form and the best musical treatment of a theme. Beautiful melodies came into his mind unbidden, and he simply wrote them down. On one occasion, while sitting in a café with some of his friends, Schubert read a German translation of Shakespeare's poem *Hark, Hark, the Lark!* A melody took shape inside him, his friends drew lines on the back of a menu, and in a few minutes Schubert had written down the complete song.

Schubert wrote so fluently that his friends may have spent more money to pay for his music paper than they did for his meals. Once a melody was on paper, however, Schubert lost interest in it, either stuffing the manuscript into a stray drawer, giving it to a friend to keep, or even burning it when fuel for the fire was scarce. Unable to keep track of his own compositions, he once praised a song that he himself had written and no longer remembered.

60. *Schubert playing for his friends.* (*Courtesy Austrian Institute, New York*)

During the early part of his career he wrote music without thinking of being paid. His friends were not so naïve. They recognized the talent of the short, chubby, nearsighted ex-choir-boy and tried to improve his financial situation. They introduced him to a famous baritone, Johann Michael Vogt, who made it his business to sing Schubert's songs on every possible occasion. Slowly, almost despite himself, Schubert was acquiring a reputation. He felt a special pleasure and pride when he learned that Beethoven, ailing and unsocial as he was, admired his music.

Vogt even managed to have a Viennese opera theater order an opera from Schubert. Unfortunately for Schubert, the music of his operas, though full of melody, was not sufficiently theatrical, and the stories were foolish and pretentious. Schubert was not destined to become wealthy writing operas.

On two occasions, he went to Hungary as a teacher for a member of the Esterhazy family. He was treated as a servant, and stayed only a few months each time, but the rest and the regular meals did him good.

In Vienna, as his reputation spread, the music he composed began to find a ready sale. But in business matters Schubert was a complete simpleton. When he made money it was almost despite himself, and he ended his chances of earning a reasonable income by selling the rights to his music for trifling sums.

The irregular life he led took its toll of his health, and from 1822 on he was never really well. He gave little thought to a future that he suspected would be a short one, and lived from day to day. Depressed by the illness that plagued him as well as by his poverty, Schubert showed, in his later works, an increasing seriousness and depth of feeling. In 1828 he died of typhus fever, the disease of the wretchedly poor, spread by lice and rats. His father and his brother, Ferdinand, arranged to have him buried near Beethoven's grave, where he would have wanted to be.

For a time it seemed that most of Schubert's music was buried with him. Then slowly it was resurrected—from old attics and music collections, from the homes of his brother and his friends, from the dusty files of musical libraries. Some of his music is still missing, and may have been burned or allowed to rot away. But we now have more than six hundred of his songs, nine symphonies, of which the *Unfinished Symphony* is most famous, many compositions for piano, and a wealth of beautiful chamber music.

We can only speculate—with regret—at what the world of music lost by his early death.

VII

THE ROMANTIC PERIOD

In the nineteenth century, the values by which men lived were transformed. National patriotism took the place of the old loyalty to duke or prince. During the French Revolution and the reign of Napoleon, Parisians and Burgundians alike became aware that they were part of a single nation. To people who found themselves herded into ugly and dirty cities, the beauties of nature acquired new importance.

In creating their works for new audiences, painters, writers, and musicians found their own values changing. No longer did musicians place great emphasis on the clear and simple forms that classical composers had bequeathed to their generation. In music, as in painting and poetry, composers had new objectives, used many new instruments, and created their own forms.

The new movements in the different arts were of many kinds, but they are often lumped together as *romantic*.

In the eyes of the older generation of music lovers, much of the new romantic music and romantic literature was in bad taste. Before the nineteenth century, individual composers like Bach and Mozart had deliberately broken some of the accepted rules of composition. Romantic composers broke the rules to proclaim their freedom. Romantic literature and romantic music revealed the author's or composer's innermost feelings. Instead of trying to create a thing of beauty, the romantic artist often seemed to be making a confession.

In music, the new freedom, like the old rules that limited freedom, did not always result in the composition of interesting or inspiring music. It did make a place for the genius of such men as Berlioz, Schumann, Mendelssohn, Chopin, Liszt, Wagner, and Brahms.

Hector Berlioz (1803–69)

To Hector Berlioz, the ideal symphony orchestra consisted, not of the few dozen players that had sufficed for Haydn and Mozart, but of four hundred sixty-five instrumentalists, accompanied by a chorus of more than three hundred voices. On one occasion, a memorial service for French heroes, he had the pleasure of hearing his great *Requiem* performed by a large symphony orchestra, chorus, four brass bands and sixteen kettledrums.

He was born in La Côte-Saint-André, a very small French town, the son of a doctor. Although as a boy he had a vivid imagination and wanted to run away to sea to visit the exotic places described in romantic tales, his parents managed to keep him at home. Here at the age of twelve, he fell madly in love with a girl of eighteen and first decided on a career in music.

His father, who gave him his first music lessons, as well as lessons in anatomy, wanted him to become a doctor too and carry on the family practice. Young Hector learned enough anatomy to be accepted by a medical school in Paris before he was eighteen. But a short exposure to the operas and concerts of the French capital convinced him that his future lay in music. He had difficulty convincing his father and was completely unsuccessful with his mother, an extremely religious woman who was certain that if he became a musician he would lose his soul to the devil.

Despite this danger, Berlioz studied music and worked hard at composition, hoping to win a government prize that would enable him to study in Rome. In order to get his music a hearing, he borrowed money and paid musicians to perform it. Unfortunately, it was too different from the music the judges wanted. During the next few years in Paris, Berlioz wrote more and more music,

61. *Hector Berlioz. (Courtesy French Embassy Press and Information Division)*

took odd jobs, learned how to get along at times on practically no food, and fell in love with two girls, more or less at the same time.

While waiting for his own music to achieve recognition, Berlioz attended the performances of works by other composers. Conductors soon realized that he was a bad man to have in the audience. At one opera, Berlioz followed the score and during a pause shouted that the orchestra was not playing the music as written. On another occasion, he started a riot because a famous solo violinist was not accompanying the ballet, as the management had promised.

Riots and fights in the audience were not uncommon in the Paris of Berlioz's day. The city was accustomed to excitement. It had lived through revolutionary changes from kingdom to republic, then to dictatorship, to an empire, and back to a kingdom again. Poets and playwrights fought for their ideas in the theaters and streets. Revolutions took place, not only in the government, but in painting, in literature, even in women's clothing. Tightly fitting skirts had given way to loosely fitting dresses. Freedom was the watchword everywhere.

In 1830, after four previous failures, Berlioz at last won the *Prix de Rome,* the Roman Prize, and prepared to leave for Italy. Of the two girls he loved, Harriet Smithson, an Irish actress and the one he was eventually to marry, would at this time have nothing to do with him. But he had managed to become engaged to the other girl, a pianist.

A month after Berlioz reached Rome, he learned that the girl to whom he was engaged had married somebody else. Enraged at the news, he set out for Paris again, planning to kill—with a single pistol shot apiece—his ex-fiancée's husband, her mother, then the girl, and finally himself. In case he ran out of bullets, he planned to poison himself. Always the actor, he intended to dress as a woman in order to gain admittance to his faithless sweetheart's house.

His trip toward Paris ran into a number of absurd obstacles, including the loss of the woman's clothing he intended to wear, and aroused the suspicions of the police, who believed that he was an agent for a revolutionary group known as Young Italy. Having had a good chance to think things over, Berlioz decided to let his intended victims live—and himself as well—and returned to Rome, where he continued his musical studies. Here he became friendly with Felix Mendelssohn, a renowned composer, and with Lord Byron, the English poet.

When Berlioz returned to France it was to fall in love again

with Harriet Smithson. He had first seen her in Paris with a
Shakespeare company, and some of his love for the Shakespearean
dramas may have been transferred to the girl he saw act in them.
He had written the *Symphonie Fantastique* to express some of
the feverish dreams of a young man like himself, and every
music lover in Paris knew that Harriet Smithson was his inspiration. Now he revised the music, and despite the hostility of some
of the critics the performance was a success. Harriet, who had
been lamed in an accident, was impressed both by the reception

62. *A cartoonist's impression of Berlioz's large orchestra includes a cannon
for good measure.* (*New York Public Library*)

63. The embittered Berlioz. (Courtesy French Embassy Press and Information Division)

of the symphony and by her suitor's impetuous courtship, and she married Berlioz in 1833.

It was not a happy marriage for either one. Harriet turned into a nagging, jealous wife (for good reason), and their life together became intolerable. They separated, and when Harriet died a number of years later, Berlioz married again, this time a singer.

He was not much luckier in love with his second wife than he had
been with Harriet.

Even during the most turbulent moments of his unhappy love
affairs Berlioz continued to study and to write music. Through
such operas as *The Trojans,* based on Virgil's poem *The Aenead,*
as well as by a book that he wrote on instrumentation, he taught
other composers what possibilities lay in the use of the brass instruments, and showed how stunning sound effects and tone
colors could be created by the orchestra. The book became famous, and several generations of composers learned from it.

Although the Parisian public was cold to his works, many outstanding musicians admired him. *Harold in Italy,* a tone poem
for solo viola and orchestra, inspired by a poem of Lord Byron,
was written at the request of Niccolò Paganini (1782–1840), a
famous violinist and composer. Although Paganini never performed the work himself, he was so moved by it that he presented
the needy Berlioz with a large sum of money.

Berlioz conducted performances of his works all over Europe,
even as far away as Russia, and in many places was received
much more warmly than in Paris. Still unable, however, to support his family by his music, he became a journalist and critic.
Outspoken in his opinions of other musicians, his articles give a
well-written and illuminating picture of musical life in Paris. He
also wrote an autobiography, which reveals his personality all the
more because he changed a few inconvenient facts and in very
human fashion slightly colored the story of his life.

It was, on the whole, an unhappy life. His only son died

64–65. *The story of his life in a cartoon. Left: Berlioz attacked by the critics
during his lifetime; right: worshiped by them after his death. (New York Public Library)*

young, his second wife also died before him. Berlioz remained alone, lonely, and embittered. Not sufficiently appreciated in his own time, he has come into his own during the past few decades. Modern audiences have been surprised by the grandeur of his *Requiem,* and of his oratorio, *L'Enfance du Crist* (*The Childhood of Christ*). Excerpts from his dramatic symphony, *The Damnation of Faust,* and from his operas are heard on concert programs.

Berlioz chose as his own epitaph Shakespeare's words about life from *Macbeth:* "It is a tale told by an idiot, full of sound and fury, signifying nothing." This once, at least, Berlioz underestimated himself. His life and work are significant in the development of music. And what magnificent sound and fury!

Felix Mendelssohn-Bartholdy
(1809–47)

Felix Mendelssohn-Bartholdy was the grandson of a famous Jewish philosopher, Moses Mendelssohn, and the son of a banker. His father, on being converted to Christianity, added the name Bartholdy, but this is often omitted, and the composer is referred to as Felix Mendelssohn.

Felix means happy, and for the greater part of his life, Mendelssohn appeared to be the happiest person in the world. Brought up in Berlin, he received a careful and thorough education. He displayed his musical ability very early, and at the age of nine, after appearing as piano soloist at a concert, he was hailed as a new Mozart. As his family was not desperately in need of money, Mendelssohn was not exploited as Mozart had been, and he enjoyed a less hectic childhood.

It was not, however, a "normal" childhood. He lived in a home whose doors were open to the outstanding musicians and writers of the time. When he was twelve years old, his friends included Goethe, the great German poet, and composers such as Weber and Rossini. It was no wonder that even as a child Mendelssohn had considerable social poise.

66. Felix Mendelssohn-Bartholdy. (New York Public Library)

He began to compose before he was eleven and in his early teens wrote considerable chamber music, much of which retains its charm and popularity. And at seventeen, inspired by his reading of Shakespeare's *A Midsummer Night's Dream,* he composed an overture whose light and graceful music transports the listener to the world of fantasy that Shakespeare created in the play.

While still playing and composing, Mendelssohn enrolled at the University of Berlin, where he took academic courses that ranged from philosophy to Latin. One of his courses was a series of lectures given by a famous philosopher, Hegel, on the nature of beauty in music. On this subject, it is likely that the student knew more than his teacher.

Mendelssohn had a tremendous respect and admiration for the almost forgotten music of Johann Sebastian Bach. He studied all the Bach scores that he could find, and became aware that the old master's works had been unfairly neglected. He was especially moved by the oratorio *The Passion According to Saint Matthew,* every note of which he knew by heart. Here, he realized, was some of the most beautiful music ever written—and no one outside Leipzig had a chance to hear it.

Many musicians who did not know Bach's music, but were aware that he wrote counterpoint, one melody sung or played against another, considered him merely a composer of mathematical exercises. Mendelssohn was determined to change this opinion. He formed a choral group, rehearsed the *St. Matthew Passion* carefully, and with the aid of Eduard Devrient, an actor and singer, arranged to conduct its first public performance. This took place in March 1829 before a full house.

It was a tremendous success. If Bach now ranks as one of the very greatest of composers, much of his reputation is due to the courage that Mendelssohn showed in reviving his music despite strong opposition. Mendelssohn, who had been raised as a Christian, was proud of his Jewish ancestry and pointed out that "it was an actor and a Jew who restored this great Christian work to the people."

He visited England to play and conduct, and after a number

of triumphant appearances, toured Scotland and Wales. He later used the musical ideas that the trip inspired in his *Scotch Symphony* and in *The Hebrides* overture, also known as *Fingal's Cave*.

He was twenty-one when the University of Berlin offered him a post as professor of music, but he preferred to travel and turned down the offer. Shortly afterward, he became musical director at Düsseldorf, but resigned to accept a similar position at Leipzig. It was here that he met Robert Schumann, who became a close friend.

Two years later he married. His home life was a happy one. Like his father, he opened his home to painters, poets, and musicians and helped such struggling composers as Chopin and Schumann. He even conducted his orchestra in the works of Berlioz, whose music he did not care for. He knew that the best critical judgment could be wrong, and he did not want to deny a hearing to a man of talent.

He visited England again, where he was almost worshiped. A master organist and pianist, he was immensely popular both with audiences and with Queen Victoria and her husband, Prince Albert.

It was for Birmingham, England, that Mendelssohn composed his oratorio *Elijah*. Mendelssohn himself conducted, and for the two and a half hours that the oratorio lasted, he noted that not one of the two thousand people in the large hall coughed or uttered a word. It was the crowning success of his career, and *Elijah* has remained popular in England ever since.

It was about this time that he wrote his only violin concerto, full of charming melodies, and the incidental music to *A Midsummer Night's Dream*. This delightful music, composed twenty years after he had written the overture, contains the familiar "Wedding March."

From about 1843, although he remained active, Mendelssohn's health began to fail. He suffered a number of strokes, and in November of 1847 he died.

After Mendelssohn's death, he and his work were attacked by

Richard Wagner, who could not forgive Mendelssohn for having been of Jewish origin. Wagner's attack was supported by other strongly anti-Semitic music groups in Germany and elsewhere. Even critics who could not be accused of anti-Semitism were intimidated and influenced by these attacks, and joined the chorus of condemnation. Especially in the years under Hitler, Mendelssohn's musical reputation suffered severely.

However, the general public has always enjoyed the music of Mendelssohn, and now that a new generation of critics has learned to listen more objectively, his reputation is once more on the rise.

Robert Schumann (1810–56)

Robert Schumann played the piano and composed at the age of six. While his father encouraged his interest in music, his mother did exactly the opposite. She wanted her son to be a lawyer, and, as the elder Schumann died when Robert was sixteen, it was her decision that counted.

Although Robert enrolled at the University of Leipzig to study law, it was not long before he was cutting all his lectures and writing music or playing the piano instead. He became a pupil of Friedrich Wieck, a well-known music teacher whose nine-year-old daughter, Clara (1819–96), was a piano prodigy.

At the University of Heidelberg, to which he transferred, Robert showed no greater interest in law than he had shown at Leipzig. This time his mother let herself be persuaded by Wieck that her son might become a great pianist, and she gave him permission to return to Leipzig and there to study music full time with Wieck.

Schumann and his friends were greatly affected by the romantic ideas expressed in the literature of the early nineteenth century, and they formed a group called "Davidsbündler" (League of David). Named after the biblical David, who slew Goliath, the group was dedicated to fighting the middle class "philistines," who had no feeling for true art. Schumann wrote essays about

67. Robert Schumann. (Courtesy German Information Center)

his friends, and even introduced himself under two names, Florestan representing his active side, and Eusebius representing the dreamer. As a composer he also expressed the characters of himself and his friends in music.

During the years that Schumann was studying, writing, and composing, Clara was becoming a charming and attractive young lady, and Schumann fell in love with her. Her father, however, did not intend to have his wonderful daughter marry a penniless musician. To make matters worse, Schumann had ruined the possibility of a career as a pianist by having used a device that was intended to strengthen his fourth finger but that permanently weakened it instead. Now he would have to make his career in music as a composer or as a critic.

Success as a critic came first. Schumann and his friends began to publish a journal called *Neue Zeitschrift für Musik,* or *New Music Magazine,* and Schumann soon became the most influential critic in Europe. For ten years, while struggling to make his own reputation as a composer, he generously used the magazine to introduce the music of other young composers.

Meanwhile, Wieck kept Clara away from Schumann by sending her on concert tours, and he started on a campaign of slander in which he accused Schumann of being a drunkard. When slander proved ineffective, he threatened to shoot Schumann. His threats were equally ineffective. Although he could prevent Clara from meeting Schumann, he could not destroy their love for each other. Clara, a highly popular concert artist, helped Schumann gain recognition as a composer by playing his piano works.

For a time Schumann thought of moving the place of publication of his magazine to Vienna, in order to give it a wider circulation. In this way he hoped to win Wieck's consent to his marriage with Clara. But Schumann's visit to Vienna brought only disappointment. Vienna was under a mad emperor, Ferdinand I, and there was no freedom for Schumann to publish his outspoken essays. In their fear of revolution, the authorities did not permit the playing of such songs as the *Marseillaise,* the French National Anthem. Schumann evaded the censors by slyly including part of the song in a piano composition, *Carnival in Vienna.*

While in Vienna, Schumann visited Franz Schubert's brother, who let him have the manuscript of Schubert's great Symphony in C. When Schumann returned to Leipzig, he presented the symphony to Mendelssohn, who gave it its first public performance.

Eventually, after going to court, Clara and Schumann were able to marry. While they were kept apart, Schumann had poured out his love in some of his most impassioned piano music. Now, in his first year of marriage, he expressed his feelings in many of his most beautiful songs. They were his wedding present to Clara.

Despite many difficulties, their marriage was successful. Schumann did not like being known chiefly as the not so famous husband of a famous pianist. In their home he and Clara agreed that *his* art must take first place, and many times Clara could not practice for fear of disturbing him while he was composing.

Other problems arose when Clara went on tour. Schumann usually accompanied her, but his own work suffered when he did so. At the same time, the tours made him realize that he was much better known and more greatly admired outside Germany than in it.

The Schumanns had eight children, and Robert, a loving father, wrote many piano pieces for them. But he had already begun to suffer from periods of depression, and at times he retreated from the world around him into a private world of his own. Medical treatment did not keep him from becoming forgetful and mentally confused. He wanted to spend more time on his work, but he had begun to hear inner voices that at times drowned out the music he tried to create. For a time he was conductor of the orchestra in Düsseldorf, but his personal problems, his vagueness, and his confusion made it impossible for him to conduct properly, and he was forced to resign.

His friendship for the young composer Johannes Brahms for a time seemed to revive his enthusiasm for living, but soon he was hearing the inner sounds again. The note A sounded continually in his mind. He was partly aware of his own illness and warned Clara, whom he loved so much, to stay away from him, for fear that he might hurt her when he was not himself.

He tried to drown himself in the Rhine River and soon had to be confined to a mental institution, where he died two years later.

Clara lived forty years more, playing her husband's compositions in concerts all over Europe. If Schumann's works—his songs, his piano music, his chamber music, and his symphonies—received the recognition they deserved, it is largely because of the devotion shown by his loyal wife.

Frédéric Chopin (1810–49)

"Hats off, gentlemen, a genius!" With these words Robert Schumann hailed Frédéric Chopin in 1831. Acclaimed a genius first by the leading European music critic, and then by many of the best-known composers and performers of the early nineteen century, Chopin appeared, at the age of twenty-one, to have achieved all a musician could ask for. A long and successful career lay ahead of him. All he had to do was compose music and perform it as he had already done.

Born near Warsaw, Chopin had been brought up in a comfortable home where everyone played at least one musical instrument. An older sister taught him to play the piano when he was four, and a local teacher carried on at a less elementary level when he was six. On his eighth birthday, he played the piano on a program given for members of the Warsaw nobility, and was so accomplished that he became, in effect, their protégé.

As he showed unusual talent for improvising and composing, his father arranged for instruction from the only teacher of composition Chopin would have in his lifetime. This teacher, Joseph Elsner was a well-known composer. He was also so good a musician that he recognized his pupil's talent to be greater than his own.

Young Chopin was a poor student of the academic subjects taught in the local lyceum, as the school of secondary education was called. He neglected all other subjects for music. In 1825 he played for the Czar of Russia, who was visiting Warsaw. Warsaw, like most of Poland, was under the czar's rule, and any sign of rebellion was brutally stamped out. On this occasion, the czar was gracious and gave Chopin a diamond ring for his playing. In

68. *The youthful Frédéric Chopin. (Courtesy French Embassy Press and Information Division)*

the same year, Chopin had the thrill of having his first composition published.

Through childhood and adolescence, Chopin stored in his mind the melodies and especially the rhythms of Polish folk songs and dances. He never forgot them, and in his later compositions he became a musical ambassador for his native land. Unfortunately, a small subjugated country like Poland was not the place where a European reputation could be made. To serve his country best, Chopin had to leave it.

In 1829 he went to Vienna and gave two highly successful concerts. He returned to Poland under the impression that a career in music now lay wide open before him. The following year, however, this same city of Vienna received him with much less warmth. One reason was the news that Poland had revolted against the czar. As the Austrian emperor also owned part of Poland, the Viennese were afraid that the revolt might spread to their section of the country.

However, the revolt was crushed, and Chopin left Vienna to try his luck in Paris, the cultural center of Europe. In 1831, when he reached Paris, he had already written his two piano concertos, and many other compositions for piano alone. He met and impressed a number of influential musicians even before he gave his first concert. Mendelssohn and Liszt were in the audience, and both they and the critics praised him highly. Nevertheless, the concert was a failure financially, and so was the following one.

Chopin was thinking about immigrating to the United States, which in 1831 was about the last place a composer of music for the piano could hope to be successful, when a Polish friend, Prince Radziwill, induced him to attend a party at the home of Baron Rothschild. Chopin had always had a snobbish liking for the nobility and at this party he won the support of the most influential people in Paris.

Slight in build and without great physical strength, Chopin had never been able to pound the piano in a large concert hall as Liszt and other popular performers did. Now he was offered invitations to perform in fashionable homes where the delicacy

69. Chopin in Paris. Photo by Pic. (Courtesy Paris Opera Museum)

and precision of his playing were at their best. Romantic in appearance as well as in his music, he also taught a number of students, mostly impressionable young girls, at a very good fee.

He now had no more financial worries, and for a few years he could enjoy his success. But his health was not good, and it was made worse when he was finally rejected by a young Polish countess to whom he had been informally engaged for two years.

Chopin's choice of the United States as a place to achieve fame and fortune was now matched by his choice of England as a place to recover his health. Unfortunately, this time no one dissuaded him. Whatever the trip to London did to make him forget his broken heart was more than balanced by the disastrous effect of the London fog and rain on his already weakened lungs. He returned to Paris after a few weeks, his health much worse than it had been when he had left.

He now fell in love with an unusual woman. Separated from her husband, Aurore Dudevant had turned to writing to support her children and herself. To escape the prejudice against women writers, she adopted the name of George Sand and became very successful, possibly because her behavior was regarded as so scandalous. To emphasize her freedom to do as she liked, she wore trousers, smoked cigars, and made no secret of her love affairs with well-known men.

Several years older than Chopin, she accepted the role of mother as well as mistress. Hoping to cure him through fresh air and sunlight, she took him to the island of Mallorca for a few months, but the weather was unco-operative, and Chopin grew worse in the damp, rainy climate. When they returned to France he was an invalid. During the years they lived together, she took good care of him, but Chopin's health continued to deteriorate. He was suffering from tuberculosis, in those days a disease for which no good treatment was known. Finally the strain on both Chopin and George Sand became too great, and they separated.

In 1848, Chopin gave a public concert, his first in six years, but the effort of playing a complete program at the piano almost killed him then and there. His health was now so bad that he could teach very few students, and he desperately needed money. He again went to England, but his musical success was accompanied by financial failure.

At the urging of a Scottish student, Jane Stirling, he went on to Scotland, where he played the piano and was the guest of several friends. Scottish hospitality was warm, but the weather was cold and wet, and the houses much the same. Chopin suffered all through his stay.

When he returned to Paris, he was completely bedridden, unable to work, and he spent on medical fees and useless treatment whatever money remained. Although Miss Stirling sent him a large gift, this was held up by the janitress of the house in which he lived, and was given to him only after considerable delay. But at this point the disease was already in its final stages, and the gift pleased Chopin chiefly because of the thoughtfulness it showed. On October 16, 1849, his doctor asked him whether he was in pain.

"No more," whispered Chopin. Then he lost consciousness, and the next day he died.

His funeral was attended by the most famous people of Paris, and the Mozart *Requiem* was sung, as he had wished.

Chopin's music is in the repertoire of every pianist, professional or amateur. In Poland, Chopin has been acclaimed for decades as the great Polish national composer. His mazurkas, études, polonaises, sonatas, waltzes, and concertos have the elegance and poetry of the romantic dreamer, without having lost the folk rhythms of his native land.

Franz Liszt (1811–86)

Women in the audience screamed and fought for a souvenir— half of a handkerchief, a few strands of hair combings, even the fabric of a chair on which their hero had sat. If their emotions were too intense they even fainted, or, to use a word that was fashionable at the time, they swooned. The scene was like that of teen-agers paying homage to a popular singer. But this was an audience of supposedly mature women in the sedate middle nineteenth century, and the man they were adoring was the most magnetic and popular pianist the concert stage had ever seen.

Franz Liszt, who was the center of this emotional storm, encouraged even the most absurd adulation. Europe was full of fine pianists, most of them unable to make a living. If Franz Liszt stood out from the crowd, it was not only because of his marvelous playing but because he had made himself the most flamboyant concert personality of the age.

Liszt was the son of a Hungarian employed as a steward by the same Esterhazy family for which Haydn had worked. He received his first music lessons from his father and showed so much talent that the local nobility contributed to his musical

70. *Franz Liszt.* (*Courtesy French Embassy Press and Information Division*)

education. In Vienna, he studied piano and composition and even played for Beethoven.

When Liszt was twelve, his father took him to Paris to be enrolled at the conservatory. He was rejected, however, by the Italian-born director, Luigi Cherubini, on the ground that he was not a native Frenchman. So he studied privately, and at thirteen he went to England, where his skill at the piano won the favor of his audiences.

About this time he even composed an opera that was performed in Paris in 1825. The composer was hailed as a young genius, although the opera was quietly forgotten.

71. An audience of women entranced by Liszt's performance, as seen by a contemporary cartoonist. (New York Public Library)

72. Niccolò Paganini, as
caricatured by Gustave Doré.
(New York Public Library)

Liszt continued to give concerts in France, Switzerland, and England and had several piano pieces published. In 1827, when his father died, leaving many debts, Liszt also accepted several students. He fell in love with one of these, the daughter of the French Minister of the Interior, but her father quickly put an end to the romance.

Liszt's reaction was a bitter one. He was good enough to be an entertainer and teacher to the nobility, but he must never forget that he came from a very much lower class, and that he was still a servant, at the beck and call of those kind enough to be his patrons.

Coming so soon after the death of his father, the incident led to Liszt's retirement from the world of music. During this period he read a great deal and became interested first in socialism and then, even more intensely, in religion. He led such a secluded life that he was reported to be dead.

As Liszt slowly recovered from his unhappiness, he met Chopin and Berlioz, whose ideas about orchestration stimulated his imagination.

However, the chief factor that helped pull him out of his depression was his attendance at a concert given by Niccolò Paganini, a violinist whose playing was so sensational that he was said to be in league with the devil. Paganini dressed in such a way that he presented an unearthly appearance, and he blandly encouraged the weird stories told about him.

Here, Liszt saw, was a man whose tremendous technical ability and remarkable personality had brought him world renown. Any pianist who wanted to stand out in the crowd of eager young musicians would need the same qualities. The personality Liszt already had; all he needed was to exaggerate those traits that would most readily attract an audience. The technique he would acquire.

For the next two years, he practiced like a demon. When he reappeared in public at the age of twenty-one, he was a phenomenally skillful pianist, with a bag of tricks to match Paganini's. After a few concerts, he had all of musical Paris in the palm of his hand.

Concert programs of the early nineteenth century were much longer than those of the present day. A performer was expected to play a concerto, many solo pieces, and finally to improvise on a theme given him.

Liszt was not the first pianist to play a program without an orchestra, but he was the first to do so successfully. Most of the time he catered to the musical ignorance of his audiences by playing dazzling piano arrangements of popular operatic arias or orchestral compositions. He was also the first to turn the piano sideways on stage. Previously, pianists had the choice of turning their backs to the audience or facing the audience across the width of the piano. Liszt turned the piano sidewise in order to exhibit his handsome profile. Seated on his bench, he would turn, transfix his listeners with a haughty stare, and toss his long hair back. Only when the audience was quiet enough to suit him would he begin to play.

As he played, he would shade the notes from barely audible sounds to loud crashes that often broke the strings of the piano. As the piano at that time had only six octaves, the strings were balanced differently from those of the present piano, with its

73. *Liszt playing for Rossini, Paganini, Victor Hugo (standing); George Sand and Alexander Dumas (seated), and the Countess D'Agoult on the floor. From a painting by Josef Danhauser. (Courtesy Austrian Institute, New York)*

seven octaves and a third, but Liszt could probably have broken the strings on any piano.

In 1833 Liszt met and fell in love with the Countess Marie d'Agoult, who was married and had two children. Two years later they eloped with the children to Switzerland, where they planned to lead the quiet life that Liszt then felt he needed.

During this period Liszt, in addition to composing, wrote a series of articles on the humiliations that musicians had to endure in their contacts with the aristocracy, and he called on all musicians to unite and tolerate no injustices or insults from officials, patrons, or anyone else.

After a while, the quiet life made Liszt restless. The countess had an income of her own, but Liszt needed money to support his mother, and he missed the adulation of his audiences. The report that a new pianist, Sigismond Thalberg, had replaced him as the idol of the public was the final straw. He returned to Paris, where he and Thalberg engaged in a battle of the keyboards.

Liszt won, and while the countess with their children (they eventually had three) stayed in Paris, Liszt traveled through Europe giving concerts. On occasion he still met with rudeness from the nobility, but now he could cope with it. When a Princess Metternich, of a family well known for its diplomats, asked him patronizingly whether he was doing good business with his concerts, he answered, "Only bankers and diplomats do good business."

In 1843 Liszt was offered a part-time position as musical director at Weimar, and a few years later gave up his tours altogether to live there. He and the countess had separated, and his new companion was the Princess Carolyne Sayn-Wittgenstein, whom he had met in Russia. The princess saw herself as a Muse inspiring the great composer, and for many years she organized Liszt's life for him. When she finally left him, Liszt took minor orders in the Catholic Church. He was henceforth known as Abbé Liszt, although he was not a priest.

At Weimar, Liszt conducted, not only the works of the masters of the past, but the compositions of composers still living, such as Schumann, Berlioz, and Wagner. He taught many talented students without charge, and in the time not devoted to helping others he composed orchestral works of his own.

Liszt was the creator of the *tone poem*, an orchestral piece inspired by a painting or literary subject. In such music as *Les Préludes* (*The Preludes*) he tried to express poetry and imagery in sound.

In 1869 his daughter, Cosima (by the Countess D'Agoult), left her husband for Richard Wagner, who was only two years younger than Liszt himself. Liszt, who had championed the music of Wagner, was greatly upset, and he was even more upset when

74. Galop Chromatique, *a caricature of Liszt in performance. Photo by Pic.*
(*Courtesy Paris Opera Museum*)

Cosima converted to Lutheranism in order to marry Wagner. For years, Liszt was estranged from both Cosima and Wagner, although they were eventually reconciled.

During the last twenty years of his life, Liszt divided his time chiefly between Weimar, Rome, and Budapest, conducting, composing, and teaching. Occasionally, he played a concert for charity. He also made a trip to London, where a Mass of his was performed, and he played for Queen Victoria, who had heard him when they were both forty-five years younger. His reception in England was a warm one, but the trip had exhausted him, and he died not long after his return.

He left behind, not only his many compositions, but a legacy of new possibilities in performance. Every pianist who presents his profile to the audience is at the same time making his bow to Liszt.

Richard Wagner (1813–83)

Richard Wagner was the supreme example of the self-centered genius. He believed that the world owed him a living, and when the world was slow to pay, he borrowed from friends and acquaintances. Most of his creditors went to their graves without having had their money returned.

Wagner felt that the great music he composed was more than enough to make up for the money he had borrowed—and for the wives, too, for sometimes he would take a man's wife just as readily as he took the man's cash.

Wagner was born in Leipzig. His father died while he was still an infant, and his mother married an actor, Ludwig Geyer, to whom Richard and his older brother and sister were devoted. As both brother and sister also went on the stage, Wagner was raised in a theatrical atmosphere. Unfortunately, Geyer died when Richard was only eight, and his mother found it impossible to care for all her children at the same time. She sent Richard to live with relatives, took him back later, and then left him again.

Although Richard was given music lessons, he never mastered any instrument. His interest in music was first aroused when he attended a performance of Weber's opera *Der Freischütz*. However, not until he heard the symphonies of Beethoven did he realize that the composition of music was to become the purpose of his life. He knew that he had much to learn and started very simply by borrowing a book on composition and following its instructions.

In obedience to his mother, he enrolled at Leipzig University, where he learned to drink and gamble but not to study. Gambling was a lifelong obsession, and much of the money he borrowed was to pay off gambling losses. As a typical student of the German universities of that day he became involved in several duels that, fortunately for him, never took place. He was too short and his eyes were too weak for him to be a good duelist.

75. *Richard Wagner in 1849.* (*Courtesy German Information Center*)

In 1831 an overture he had written was performed to the boos and laughter of a Leipzig audience. He was not too greatly discouraged, and later a symphony of his was well received.

About this time his actor brother got him a job as chorusmaster in Würzburg. The position served a double purpose; it paid him a salary and it took him out of Saxony, where he was in danger of being drafted into the army. In 1834 he became musical director of a theatrical company in the small city of Lauchstädt in order to be near Minna Planer, an actress in the company. It took two years for Wagner to persuade her to marry him.

One unimportant musical position now followed another in Wagner's life, along with a trail of unpaid debts. When he lost his position as conductor of the opera in Riga, Latvia, he, Minna, and their enormous Newfoundland dog had to cross the border secretly.

Once out of range of their Latvian creditors, the Wagners took ship for England. Violent storms made the journey, which ordinarily required a week, last almost a month. The wild seas gave Wagner the idea for his future opera *The Flying Dutchman.*

England was only a temporary stop on the way to Paris. Wagner arrived at the French capital with letters of introduction from Giacomo Meyerbeer, whom we have already noted as an extremely successful composer of opera. But despite the cordiality of Meyerbeer and other established composers, Wagner found life in Paris rather difficult. He earned a meager living writing articles, translating, and doing routine musical jobs. In the hope of making a fortune from an operatic production, he spent money recklessly and went heavily into debt. When the theater failed, his creditors had him imprisoned. On his release, he and Minna returned to Germany.

In 1842 he had his first operatic success with *Rienzi.* A few months later, however, *The Flying Dutchman* was badly produced and was a failure. But neither success nor failure put much money in Wagner's pockets. In a subsequent production, *The Flying Dutchman* was well received by the public, but the critics savagely attacked it, and it had only a short run.

In 1848 revolutions broke out in many European countries, and Wagner gave the German revolution his support—but only in his writing. Although he exhorted others to fight, he prudently avoided the fighting himself. Nevertheless, when the revolution failed, he had to flee Germany.

In Sweden, where he took refuge, he had the leisure to develop his theories about art and opera. Like Gluck a century before, he believed that music and libretto must form a unity. What Wagner wanted was not opera, but *music drama*. To attain unity, the composer must not only write his own music to his own libretto, he must plan all stage action and design all the sets.

As a former revolutionary on the way to becoming a German superpatriot, Wagner believed the German people superior to any other, especially to the French and Italians. Even his most cheerful music drama, *The Mastersingers of Nürnberg*, calls for the leadership of the Germans over the "inferior" Latin peoples.

After a search for themes that would express both his ideas about music drama and his feelings about Germany, Wagner selected the Nibelungen myths. Apparently he saw no conflict between his ideas about German superiority and the fact that the old myths presented the German gods, who were presumably superior even to the German people themselves, as liars and cheats.

While Wagner was occupied with his musical ideas, his marriage was falling apart. In 1851, after years of unhappiness, Minna finally left him. Soon after, Wagner met a couple, the Wesendoncks, who became devoted friends and patrons. In Mathilde Wesendonck, Wagner found a new love, if only a temporary one. She inspired him to write *Tristan and Isolde,* one of the most magnificent expressions of love in all music.

In Weimar, Liszt produced Wagner's *Lohengrin* and helped Wagner in any way he could. In Paris, however, where Wagner's *Tannhäuser* was performed in 1861, Wagner encountered hostility. Parisian operagoers demanded ballet in their operas, and, when Wagner finally yielded to the extent of inserting one, he made the mistake of putting it in the first act. As the influential members of the opera audience never arrived before the second act of any opera, and therefore missed the ballet altogether, the opera house was soon in an uproar, with the latecomers demanding a ballet that had already been given.

Wagner, increasingly bitter, blamed Meyerbeer, who had formerly interceded in his behalf. Wagner repeatedly showed his anti-Semitism, singling out for special condemnation the people who had helped him. He also attacked Mendelssohn, despite the fact that the latter had been raised as a Lutheran and was now dead. In his anti-Semitism, Wagner exhibited a lack of consistency whenever consistency conflicted with his own needs. For instance, when he had his own theater in Bayreuth, he selected a Jewish conductor, Hermann Levi, to lead the performances.

Wagner's hatred was not limited to Jews. Possibly because of his experiences in Paris, he developed a great hatred for France, and during the Franco-Prussian War, in 1870, called for the destruction of Paris by burning it to the ground. In this he anticipated the feelings of his worshiper, Adolf Hitler, who had the same idea.

By now, despite the failure of some of his operas, Wagner's musical reputation was well established. He toured Europe, making disciples as well as enemies, but nowhere did he find operatic impresarios who would let him present operas exactly as he wished.

And then a miracle happened. The young King Ludwig II of Bavaria, a devoted supporter, offered him a theater in Munich, a fine salary, and the freedom to put on his music dramas exactly as he wished. The king, always eccentric, and later completely mad, was destined to be put away in an asylum and to end his life by drowning. But for a number of years he was almost a servant of Wagner's and took the latter's advice on politics as well as music.

In Munich, Wagner worked in peace, except for a few storms that he himself stirred up. He had fallen in love again, this time with Cosima von Bülow, daughter of Liszt and wife of Hans

76. Richard Wagner in Heaven, *a contemporary cartoon, pokes fun at Wagner's arrogance: 1. Cherubs blow tubas while Beethoven holds his ears in pain; 2. Wagner teaches Mozart and Beethoven his true harmonies; 3. Wagner roasts Jacques Offenbach, who had the misfortune to be both a successful composer and a Jew; 4. Angels fetch him silk underclothes; 5. A complete performance of his trilogy is a daily treat; 6. A cherub beats the drum in praise of Wagner, who is seated on a heavenly throne in the guise of Wotan, ruler of the Norse gods. (New York Public Library)*

von Bülow, a conductor and pianist who had been one of his closest musical allies. Cosima had three children by Wagner before she divorced Von Bülow and married Wagner.

Cosima made Wagner's work her whole life, and he appreciated her devotion. When their son, Siegfried, was born, he composed a charming piece for small orchestra, the *Siegfried Idyll,* which he had performed at their home as a surprise for Cosima.

Wagner's behavior, especially a denial that he was involved with Cosima, upset King Ludwig, and Wagner had to leave Munich. But Wagner and the king corresponded, and the king continued his financial support.

For many years, Wagner had been working on *The Ring of the Nibelungs,* a cycle of four music dramas. With the help of King Ludwig and other supporters, the first performances were given in August 1876 in a theater especially built for Wagner in Bayreuth, Germany.

The production was unprecedented in many ways. The entire *Ring* took almost thirteen hours to perform and was given on four successive nights. The audience of emperors, kings, princes, famous musicians, and friends and enemies of Wagner was dazzled by the beauty of the music, as well as stupefied by its unending flow.

The performance made Wagner world-famous, but it did not yet rid him of his creditors. Many of Wagner's debts not due to gambling resulted from his ideas of luxurious living. His rooms were covered with silks and velvets, he could tolerate only certain colors, and he indulged himself in such pleasures as expensive imported foods and rare flowers.

Wagner emerged from a period of deep thinking with a new mystical approach to religion. His final music drama, *Parsifal,* is a very lengthy work about the Knights of the Holy Grail. *Parsifal* contains music as beautiful as any he ever wrote, and it is usually performed during Easter week. Although it is given in opera houses rather than churches, it has become traditional for audiences who attend it not to applaud.

Wagner was now old and ill, and in 1882 he and Cosima went to Venice in the hope that the warm weather would improve his

77. Wagner in his later years. (Courtesy German Information Center)

health. Instead, he became steadily worse and suffered several heart attacks before the one that finally killed him. The entire musical world, even his enemies, mourned him.

Did he succeed in creating a truly unified music drama? His ideas about the unity of words and music have influenced many operatic composers, but it is questionable whether he achieved in his own works the complete unity he sought. It is his magnificent music that keeps his work alive, not the silly and pretentious librettos of which he was so proud.

In addition to his legacy of great music, he left another of hatred. During the years of Hitler's rule, the German nazis embraced Wagner's super-German nationalism and his anti-Semitism and revered him as their cultural god. With their downfall, we can more readily accept the power and passion of his music, and disregard the dangerous and hateful aspects of his complex personality.

Johannes Brahms (1833–97)

Johannes Brahms grew up in a Hamburg slum, one of three children born to a struggling musician and his seamstress wife. The elder Brahms played any instrument from double bass to horn, in any place from a tavern to a military band. Young Johannes, who was exposed to all sorts of music, showed a special interest in the piano, and he was given lessons from the age of seven. His talent impressed his teacher so greatly that the latter arranged for lessons with a more prominent teacher, who taught Johannes—without charge—composition as well as piano.

At thirteen Johannes used his music to help support his family. He played the piano in beer halls and cheap restaurants and at dances, usually starting late at night and ending in the early morning. The late hours, the sordid environment, the daily lessons, and the continual practicing combined to exhaust the young pianist. He became thin, pale, and nervous.

At this point, he was offered a position as piano teacher to a young girl whose family spent the summer in the country. Two summers in which he enjoyed fresh air, good food, and a relaxed atmosphere made a healthy young man of Brahms, and he was always grateful to the family that treated him so well.

By sixteen he had determined to be a composer. He educated himself by reading whenever he was not accompanying, teaching, or doing any of the small musical jobs he needed to keep from starving.

At twenty Brahms met a young Hungarian violinist, Edward Remenyi, whom he accompanied on a concert tour. They played for

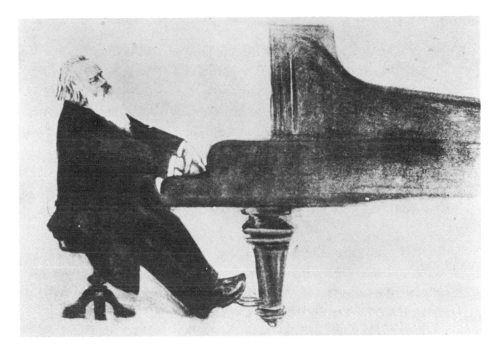

78. *Johannes Brahms at the piano.* (*Courtesy Austrian Institute, New York*)

the King of Hanover, but the police discovered that Remenyi had been involved in a revolution in Hungary, and the two young musicians were expelled from Hanover.

At Weimar they met Franz Liszt, who was greatly impressed by Brahms's talents. Brahms, never a diplomat, failed to return the compliment and is said to have fallen asleep while Liszt was playing for him. His bored attitude upset Remenyi, who respected Liszt's music, admired him as a fellow Hungarian, and needed his help. Remenyi and Brahms parted company.

Another famous violinist, Joseph Joachim, came to the rescue, and he and Brahms gave a concert together. The profits enabled Brahms to tour Germany and meet other musicians. In Düsseldorf, where he met Robert and Clara Schumann, he felt an especial warmth. Schumann tried to find him a publisher and hailed him as a genius, as he had hailed Chopin. This well-meant praise made people expect too much of Brahms, but several published piano pieces and songs were successful, and his musical reputation continued to grow.

In January of 1854, the Schumanns visited Brahms in Hanover, and the three spent a wonderful week together that Brahms never forgot. Only a month later however, Schumann attempted to commit suicide and had to be put into an asylum. Brahms rushed to Clara and the children, and his companionship helped her survive the agony of Schumann's illness and, later, of his death.

Brahms, who was in love with Clara Schumann and wanted to be near her, stayed on in Düsseldorf, teaching music. Clara was fourteen years older than Brahms, but she was a beautiful and gifted woman who had made many sacrifices for her husband's sake, and Brahms's love for her was matched by his admiration. Clara, on the other hand, felt more like a mother to him, and she insisted that he return to his neglected career. She listened to his music, she advised and criticized, and she played his compositions in her concerts. Their mutual devotion lasted till the end of their lives.

In the years that followed Schumann's death, Brahms was the victim of verbal attacks by Liszt and Wagner partisans, who proclaimed them the finest composers and performers of German music. Brahms and Joachim ridiculed these pretensions, and the infuriated Wagnerites did all they could to prevent Brahms from obtaining a good musical position.

Despite the attacks upon him, Brahms continued to turn out increasingly beautiful music. When he was thirty he left Hamburg for Vienna, where he expected to stay only a short time. He was so well received in Vienna by musicians and writers, as well as by the general public, that he remained there for the rest of his life.

His *Hungarian Dances* and other piano pieces had brought him the sneers of Wagner, who called him a "Jewish czardas player." Now, as they became increasingly popular, they also brought him a good income. In addition, he profited by going on several concert tours with Joachim. But most of his time was spent on composing.

Brahms was a romantic composer, but he was not attracted to

79. *Johannes Brahms.* (*Courtesy Austrian Information Service*)

the tone poem. He felt that music should not attempt to tell a
story or describe a picture. His ideal was the classical symphonic
form, music created for its own sake. Within this form, the composer could best communicate his own emotions.

Brahms composed with great care and destroyed whatever failed
to meet his own high standards. Though he knew his own worth,
he was modest in comparing himself with such masters as Beethoven. His admirers had no such modesty. They coined the phrase
"The Three B's" in order to link Bach and Beethoven with Brahms
as three immortals.

When he was about forty, Brahms became conductor of the
Vienna Choral Society and introduced works by Bach and Handel
that had long been forgotten. By now the Viennese food had left
its mark upon him, and he was quite heavy. Still clean-shaven, he

80. *Choral societies were active all over Europe. A cartoon of one such society.* (*New York Public Library*)

dressed very carelessly and always had a cigar in his mouth. His only personal luxury was collecting original manuscript scores of the great composers. Not until he was about fifty did he begin to grow the beard that hides his face in so many portraits.

His early days of playing in beer halls and restaurants had

81. Brahms with Johann Strauss, Jr. (Courtesy Austrian Information Service)

taught him that music need not be pretentious to be good. He once autographed the fan of a daughter of Johann Strauss, the "Waltz King," by jotting down the first few notes of the *Blue Danube Waltz* and adding, "Unfortunately, not by Johannes Brahms."

With little formal education, he was offered honorary degrees by several universities, including Cambridge, in England. He was a worthy recipient of these degrees, apart from his music, for he had acquired informally an education that not many university graduates could match.

Honors of all kinds came to him. His native Hamburg, which for so many years had ignored his existence, finally gave him the keys to the city.

As he grew older, he became ever sloppier and more careless in his clothes. They were never pressed, and sometimes different articles were held together by pins. He also became ruder and grumpier. On leaving a social gathering, he once said, "If there's anyone here whom I've forgotten to insult, I ask him to forgive me."

In his work he remained as careful and painstaking as ever, and toward young musicians struggling to gain a foothold, he

82. *Brahms, as seen in silhouette. (New York Public Library)*

was unusually generous. Among those he helped was Antonin Dvořák.

In 1896 Clara Schumann died. Brahms was already a sick man, and although he realized that Clara was seventy-seven years old, he never recovered fully from the shock of this loss. In April 1897 he himself died of cancer. Four symphonies, concertos, a number of sonatas and piano pieces, and many beautiful works of chamber music—all provide abiding evidence of his genius.

VIII

THE LATER ROMANTICS

Among the composers who fell under Wagner's spell, three names have most meaning for music lovers today: Anton Bruckner, Hugo Wolf, and Gustav Mahler. All three were frustrated in their struggles for public recognition.

Anton Bruckner (1824–96)

Bruckner, an extremely religious man, was the oldest of eleven children of a schoolmaster. Like Haydn, Schubert, and Rossini, he too became a choirboy. Almost completely self-taught, he was a fine organist and was appointed to the Cathedral of Linz. His reputation as organist and composer of church music brought him invitations to perform in Paris, London, and Vienna, where he was acclaimed.

In his mid-forties, after becoming acquainted with Wagner's works, he left his church position and went to Vienna, where he taught and composed. In 1867, he suffered a nervous breakdown, and when he recovered, his religious, almost mystical feelings were stronger than ever. He tried to express his exalted emotions in nine massive symphonies, which he wrote and rewrote. Unfortunately they seemed to exhaust rather than inspire his audiences. They felt that sitting for over an hour and a quarter during the performance of a single symphony made the music a punishment rather than a joy.

Bruckner and the supporters of Brahms carried on a constant

83. Anton Bruckner. (Courtesy American Information Service)

feud, and Bruckner appealed to the emperor for aid. The emperor did give him an income as well as an apartment, but could not give him the acclaim and acceptance he sought. Today his symphonies, although still not very popular, are being heard oftener than they ever were during his lifetime.

Hugo Wolf (*1860–1903*)

The life of Hugo Wolf was short and tragic. He attended the Vienna Conservatory but was expelled before he could graduate. Unable to earn a living as a musician, he, like Berlioz and Schumann, turned to the career of music critic. This did not increase his popularity, and, as an admirer of Wagner in a city that adored Brahms, he made many enemies. Wolf wrote an opera, a quartet, and many beautiful songs, for which he is best known. His aim was to do for the song what Wagner did for the opera libretto, to use the music to express the poet's ideas and feelings. His more than two hundred fifty songs are among the most perfect musical evocations of poetry, but, like the rest of his works, they did not receive an impartial hearing, and their failures intensified his feelings of depression. He would compose with intense concentration for days, and then he would fall into a despondent mental state where he could do nothing. It was only after his death in an insane asylum, where he spent seven years, that his songs became part of the vocal repertoire.

Gustav Mahler (*1860–1911*)

Today, the best known of the group is Gustav Mahler. Born in Bohemia, the son of a poor Jewish shopkeeper, he was so talented that he played the accordion at four, studied the piano at six, and was enrolled at the Vienna Conservatory when he was only fifteen. For a time he was a student of Bruckner. An outstanding pianist, he preferred to earn his living as a composer, but with so little success that he turned to conducting. His high standards of performance delighted audiences in Budapest, Prague, Hamburg, and London, but were less warmly received by his colleagues. Mahler was a single-minded, impatient, and high-strung man, regarded as a tyrant by singers and instrumentalists because

84. *Gustav Mahler.* (*Courtesy Austrian Information Service*)

of his unrelenting demand for their best efforts. Brahms, who was
not enthusiastic about Mahler's gifts as a composer, was most enthusiastic about his talents as a conductor and opera director.

Mahler's symphonies all dealt in one way or another with the
tragedy of man's life on earth, and it was possibly because of the
same feeling of desperation that in 1895 he became a convert to
Catholicism. Tragic as they are, however, his symphonies are not
depressing. He used many folk melodies, weaving them with
great skill into the pattern of orchestral instruments. In addition
to nine completed symphonies, he composed a song cycle for
voice and orchestra based on a collection of German folk poems
known as *The Youth's Magic Horn,* as well as other works for
voice and orchestra. Four of his symphonies call for enormous
orchestras and large choral groups, as well as vocal soloists. As
in the case of Berlioz, these great demands on musical resources
for a single performance made it difficult and expensive to perform his works.

Although Mahler was in great demand as a conductor, he did
not become a wealthy man. He knew that he had heart disease
and tried desperately to make enough money to provide for his
wife and child. Because of this, he accepted a position as con-

85. Mahler conducting. (New York Public Library)

ductor at the Metropolitan Opera House, in New York, and, at the same time, undertook to conduct the New York Philharmonic Orchestra. After he collapsed during a concert, he returned to Vienna, to die an unhappy man, embittered by the knowledge that his works had not gained the acceptance they deserved.

Changes in public and critical taste have led to a greater appreciation of his romantic spirit, his skilled and unusual use of orchestral instruments, and his musical treatment of folk melodies.

Richard Strauss (1864–1949)

Richard Strauss, born in Munich, achieved public recognition for his orchestral tone poems while still a young man, and he became world famous for his operas. *Der Rosenkavalier* (*The Knight of the Rose*), a comic opera, is loved by opera audiences, as its

86. *Richard Strauss conducting.* (*Courtesy German Information Center*)

sensuous waltzes are loved by concert audiences. His opera *Salome* created a scandal in 1905 because of its discordant music and its presumably immoral "Dance of the Seven Veils." By to-day's standards, neither the music nor the dance is even mildly shocking.

Unlike so many other composers, he was also a very good businessman. He himself handled all financial details of performance and publication of his works, and he became a wealthy man.

The compositions of his later life lack the appeal of his earlier operas and tone poems. In his old age his reputation was shadowed by his continued residence in Germany during the Hitler years, and by his acceptance of honors from the nazi government. However, when the nazis wished to replace Mendelssohn's immortal music for *A Midsummer Night's Dream* with pure "Aryan" music, Strauss refused to co-operate.

IX

THE RISE OF NATIONALISM

We have seen how the French Revolution and the military triumphs of the French armies under Napoleon stimulated the growth of nationalism. This new form of patriotism developed at different rates and for different reasons throughout Europe. In France, nationalism meant the defense of the new order against the attacks of feudalism; in Russia, it meant the defense of a backward and feudal empire against the attacks of the French invaders. In Germany, it meant the growing tendency toward union of a number of states into one large and powerful state under a central government. In Italy, Poland, and Czechoslovakia, nationalism grew out of the resentment that the Italians, Poles, Czechs, and Slovaks felt against their foreign oppressors, whether French, Austro-Hungarian, German, or Russian.

The various movements for liberation from foreign tyranny emphasized the importance of the native cultures against the cultures of the hated rulers. Many composers shared these feelings but nonetheless went to Paris or Vienna, the centers of musical inspiration. Chopin's music, for example, reflected the Polish folk music that he had heard as a child, but it remained more romantic than Polish. In other countries, however, composers consciously attempted to break away from the dominance of foreign music and to write music that would reflect the national spirit.

Nowhere was this spirit in music more evident than in Russia.

RUSSIA

The largest European country, Russia was isolated from the West for many centuries. Not until Peter the Great (1672–1725) tried to modernize his vast empire did Western music filter in. As the Russian aristocrats began to ape the life of aristocrats in Western European courts, they discovered the charms of formal music, especially in Italian opera and French ballet.

Catherine the Great (1729–96), a German princess who became Czarina of Russia, invited many well-known Italian composers and performers to her court. Few men wanted to leave such pleasant cities as Paris and Rome for the bleak winters and unexciting life of Moscow and St. Petersburg, and Catherine paid them well. Among the visitors were Domenico Cimarosa (1749–1801), who wrote *The Secret Marriage*, and Giovanni Paisiello, (1741–1816), Rossini's rival.

Foreign musicians brought with them the works of Gluck, Haydn, and Mozart and inspired the native Russian composers to imitate these masters. Most native composers were talented serfs who had been educated by their noble owners and, in some cases, liberated.

The patriotic fervor that seized the Russians following the defeat of Napoleon's invasion in 1812 led to an interest in Russian history, life, and legends. The poet Alexander Pushkin, who was familiar with the works of Shakespeare, Voltaire, Molière, and Byron, led a movement to develop a native Russian literature. Pushkin's friend, Michael Glinka, led a similar movement in music.

Michael Glinka (1804–57)

Glinka, the son of a wealthy landowner, became a professional musician over his family's objections. As a young man, he held a minor position in the government in St. Petersburg, and his life was idle and aimless. Glinka did as his friends did: he went to parties, flirted, drank, and gambled. He even played a minor role in one of the numerous conspiracies against the czar, but managed to clear himself with the police.

Glinka then went abroad for his health, but he also took ad-

87. *Michael Glinka.*
(*New York Public Library*)

vantage of the opportunity to study music in Germany and Italy,
and to visit Spain, where he was fascinated by the folk music and
dance rhythms. Later he wrote music that utilized Spanish melodies and rhythms. Many other Russian composers after him were
also drawn to Spanish music, perhaps because so much of it, like
Russian music, reveals an Oriental influence.

When Glinka returned to Russia in 1834, he was an accomplished musician. His first opera, originally called *Ivan Susanin*,
was renamed *A Life for the Czar* in order to flatter that monarch, and dealt with the heroic feat of a simple soldier who saves
the czar's life. Most of the music was in the Italian style, but
Glinka also included Russian and Polish folk melodies and
rhythms.

His next opera, *Russlan and Ludmilla*, based on a Russian

fairy tale, was more authentically Russian in its melodies and harmonies. However, although the music was beautiful, the opera was a failure. Unhappy at its poor reception, he returned to Western Europe. The warmth with which he was greeted by Liszt, Berlioz, and Meyerbeer could not compensate for the coldness of Glinka's reception in his native land. Homesick for Russia, he became more eccentric and embittered as his health grew worse, and when he died, in Berlin, his only companions were the numerous birds and rabbits with which he had surrounded himself.

Glinka had a devoted sister, Ludmilla Shestakova, who made it her mission in life to promote the music of her dead brother, as well as of the young composers who followed in his footsteps. Her home became the center of a group of young amateur musicians known as The Five.

The Five

Mili Balakirev (1837–1910), the organizer and teacher of the group, was the son of a poor nobleman. He was educated in music with the assistance of a wealthy patron. A student of physics and mathematics, he eventually decided on a professional musical career. He was greatly attracted by music of the East, and his compositions have an Oriental flavor.

The second member, César Cui (1835–1918), was an army officer who ended his military career as a general. The author of a book on military engineering, Cui also composed ten operas and much other music, and for a number of years he was an influential critic. He was the least important member of The Five, and his music is now hardly ever played.

Number Three was probably the most important member of The Five. He was Modest Mussorgsky, whose short life profoundly affected the course of Russian music.

Modest Mussorgsky (1839–81) came from a wealthy landowning family. However, his grandmother had been a serf, and all his life

88. Modest Mussorgsky. (New York Public Library)

he had a feeling of identification with the peasants. He received the usual upper-class education of the time, including piano lessons. He learned so rapidly that at the age of nine he could play a concerto for his parents' guests. He continued to study piano but never had formal instruction in composition.

At seventeen, he joined a guards regiment composed of aristocratic young men whose main occupations were drinking, gambling, and women-chasing. Mussorgsky followed their example so well that he was on the way to being an alcoholic before he reached twenty.

It was his interest in music that saved him from becoming as useless as his fellow guardsmen. When he was twenty he resigned from the army to devote himself completely to music. He began to study orchestration with Balakirev, and also wrote a number of songs and other compositions.

When Czar Alexander II freed the serfs in 1861, Russia took a giant step into modern times. For some of the landowners, however, the loss of their serfs was disastrous. Mussorgsky's family was one of the unlucky ones, and Mussorgsky was forced to take a menial job as a clerk in order to support himself. He now had time for composition only in the evenings and on Sundays. He used this time to write songs, in which he gradually moved away from romantic themes and aimed at what he called "realism." "It is the people I want to portray as they are," he said, and he tried to convey, in music, the humor, sorrow, and flavor of peasant speech.

Mussorgsky himself could hardly be regarded as peasant-like. Very sociable and witty, he was good company whether he spoke, sang, or played the piano. His manners were those of the well-bred aristocrat. In early life, he made an attractive appearance, spoiled somewhat by a reddish nose that an artist friend, Repin, described as potato-shaped. Mussorgsky blamed the red nose on frostbite suffered while in the army. It is likely, however, that his heavy drinking also contributed to its color.

When he was about thirty he began work on an opera based on Pushkin's drama *Boris Godunov*. Boris was a czar who reached the throne in 1598 through murder, and was then, according to Pushkin, destroyed by his own conscience. Mussorgsky completed the first draft in six months, but after a long delay, the opera directors rejected it. Mussorgsky revised the opera and submitted it again. After another delay, the opera was produced in 1874 and was a success, despite the fact that many of the members of the audience as well as the critics failed to understand it.

Mussorgsky's choice of harmonies, his use of the orchestra and of human voices, his unusual and unexpected presentation of the Russian people as a force in Russian history, and his psychological insight into the characters made *Boris Godunov* one of the most stirring of all operas. These very qualities were probably responsible for its being dropped from the repertory of the St. Petersburg Royal Opera Company, very likely on orders from the court.

Although disheartened by the difficulties with *Boris,* he started work on two other operas. *Khovanchina* dealt with another incident in Russian history, while *The Fair at Sorochinsk* was a more earthy, lusty peasant story. He completed neither work, and his friend Rimsky-Korsakov orchestrated them after Mussorgsky's death. He did complete *Pictures at an Exhibition,* a group of very descriptive piano pieces, and the tone poem *A Night on Bald Mountain,* a musical evocation of a witches' sabbath.

Mussorgsky's struggles with the censors, with poverty, and with the wretched job he had, combined with disappointments in his musical career, led to greater reliance on alcohol to make life tolerable. When his government job came to an end, he became an accompanist for a singer who toured Russia. By now he was no longer a dapper young man. He was heavy and bloated from drinking, and he had become careless in his dress. Yet he was highly valued as an accompanist and was always willing to contribute his services for charity performances.

On one occasion a famous Italian singer offered to sing at a charity concert but asked for a rehearsal first. He had never met Mussorgsky and was unaware that the latter was drunk. Mussorgsky's friends assured the singer that Mussorgsky, too "busy" to meet with him, would play an excellent accompaniment at the concert itself.

By some miracle, they managed to get Mussorgsky to the concert hall in one of his rare sober intervals. However, a backstage buffet held a wide assortment of liquid refreshments, and by the time he sat down at the piano, he was far from sober. The singer made matters worse when he revealed that he had a sore throat and asked Mussorgsky to transpose the unfamiliar music into a different key. Drunk or sober, Mussorgsky could play and transpose at sight brilliantly, and the performance was a great success.

Mussorgsky's music was hailed outside Russia by influential musicians such as Liszt, but Mussorgsky himself could not afford to leave Russia. While The Five remained together, he felt that his friends would to some extent make up for the family he lacked, but in later years The Five drifted apart, and Mussorgsky felt himself completely alone and deserted. He collapsed completely. However, several friends still remained, and they arranged for his admission to a hospital where he could receive proper care. But the years of alcohol and neglect had done their work, and Mussorgsky died a few days after his forty-second birthday.

Glinka's sister expressed the feelings of all who knew him when she said, "He will live forever, not only as the author of *Boris,* but as a rare, kind, honest, and gentle man."

The fourth member of The Five, Alexander Borodin (1833–87), was a physician and a professor of chemistry at the Medical School in St. Petersburg. He too came from a noble family, and from childhood on showed great interest in both music and science. After he started to teach, he had time to compose only when he was on vacation or too ill to attend his classes, and his musical friends would greet him with the hope that he was in bad health.

Like Mussorgsky, Borodin had no formal training in composition. Nevertheless, he wrote several symphonies, songs, and a tone poem, *In the Steppes of Central Asia.* His major work, the opera *Prince Igor,* based on a Russian hero who was partly historical and partly legendary, was left uncompleted, and was prepared for performance after his death by Rimsky-Korsakov. The opera contains a wild and barbaric ballet, the *Polovtsian Dances.* Melodies from *Prince Igor,* as well as from his enchanting second String Quartet were made even more widely known when they

89. *Alexander Borodin.*
(*New York Public Library*)

were arranged as the score of an American musical comedy, *Kismet.*

Borodin's personal life was completely disorganized. His home was literally "open house" at all times, and dozens of relatives, friends, and students visited or lived there. Borodin and his wife both ate at odd hours, and when they moved to a new apartment, cartons and suitcases filled with their personal belongings were scattered everywhere, to be opened when the mood struck them. To add to the confusion, the Borodin apartment became a haven for stray cats who, like the guests, needed no invitation to move in.

No matter how great the uproar, Borodin appeard undisturbed. His laboratory adjoined his apartment and he moved from one to the other, seemingly without losing the thread of his musical or scientific thoughts.

He made several trips to Western Europe for scientific purposes, and took advantage of the occasions to meet Liszt and other musicians who admired his work. Unfortunately, he was never in good health, and one night, after enjoying himself at a party, he collapsed and died of a heart attack.

Born into an aristocratic family with a long tradition of naval service, Nicholas Rimsky-Korsakov (1844–1908) was enrolled in the Naval Cadets when he was twelve years old. At about this time, too, he began to study the piano seriously. When he was seventeen, he became a student of Balakirev but was forced to discontinue his studies when he left on a cruise that lasted three years.

On returning to shore, he resumed his work on music and completed a symphony and a number of songs. He even tried his hand at an opera, but was aware of its weaknesses, some of them arising from his lack of musical knowledge. At the age of twenty-seven, however, he was offered a professorship in composition and instrumentation at the St. Petersburg Conservatory. Although he knew less about the subject than some of his pupils, he accepted the position, intending to teach himself while teaching his classes. In a few years he was a master of the technique of composing for the orchestra, and he wrote a book on the subject.

Rimsky-Korsakov wrote many symphonic works and fourteen operas, often based on Russian legends and fairy tales, as well as on tales of Pushkin and the writer Nikolai Gogol. His fairy-tale operas were not meant only for children. One of them, *The Golden Cockerel,* so obviously ridiculed the rulers of Russia that the censors refused permission to have it performed.

During an unsuccessful revolution in 1905, brought on by Russia's disastrous defeat in the Russo-Japanese War, Rimsky-Korsakov defended students involved in the uprising and was, as

90. *Nicholas Rimsky-Korsakov.* (*New York Public Library*)

a result, fired from the conservatory. As part of his punishment, performances of his works were forbidden, but there was so much protest that after a year he was reappointed to the conservatory and his works were performed again.

Rimsky-Korsakov's symphonic work *Scheherazade*, inspired by *Tales of the Arabian Nights*, has long been one of the most popular compositions in the orchestral literature. The censors found no political significance in it. They found a great deal, in his opera *Christmas Eve*, after the grand dukes of Russia complained that the opera insulted their grandmother, the Empress Catherine.

Rimsky-Korsakov married, had children, and apparently lived the closest to a normal life of all the members of The Five. Balakirev and Cui outlived him, but their influence faded after Rimsky-Korsakov's death in 1908.

Peter Ilyitch Tchaikovsky
(1840–93)

The son of a well-to-do mine inspector, Tchaikovsky was one of six children. He attended a law school and became a clerk in the Ministry of Justice. When he went abroad at the age of twenty-one, he became very much interested in music, and on his return to St. Petersburg he enrolled in the Conservatory of Music. Although he showed talent, he was too nervous to pass his final oral examination. Nevertheless, when Nicholas Rubinstein, brother of the famous Anton, established a music school in Moscow, he invited Tchaikovsky to teach there.

Tchaikovsky's salary was a small one, and, to make up for it, Rubinstein allowed him to live rent-free in the apartment he himself occupied as director of the school.

The move to Moscow had removed Tchaikovsky from the influence of the nationalist Five, and he found himself drawn to the romantic music of Western Europe. He had already begun to compose, but he was very critical of his own work and destroyed most of it even after it had been performed. About this time, Balakirev suggested to him that Shakespeare's *Romeo and Juliet* would make an excellent subject for a symphonic tone poem. It did. Tchaikovsky's *Romeo and Juliet* has been popular with audiences since its premiere in 1870. The tragedy of the two lovers who were victims of their families' feud is expressed in music that evokes the emotions of the play.

In 1874 he wrote his first piano concerto, dedicated to Nicholas Rubinstein, who did not like it. Hurt and angered, Tchaikovsky withdrew the dedication to Rubinstein and addressed it to Von Bülow instead. Rubinstein later changed his mind about the con-

91. *Peter Ilyitch Tchaikovsky. (New York Public Library)*

certo and performed it with great success. It was played all over Europe and the United States and did a great deal to make Tchaikovsky famous. However, it did not bring him much of an income, and his salary, still low, did not enable him to live very well.

Rubinstein, aware of Tchaikovsky's desperate need of money, spoke to a wealthy widow, Madame Nadejda von Meck, and suggested that she commission some compositions from him. Madame von Meck, about forty-seven years old, was as shy and unhappy in her own way as Tchaikovsky was in his. Music was the one great passion of her life, and although she was ill at ease in meeting people face to face, she was more courageous in her letters.

She and Tchaikovsky began a friendship by mail only. Madame von Meck insisted that they must never meet in person, and Tchaikovsky was happy to agree with her. This arrangement left them freer to express their hopes and fears about life and music. Later she lent him money and gave him a pension of about three thousand dollars a year so that he might compose in peace of mind.

In 1877 his ballet *Swan Lake* was performed. Now one of the most beloved ballet scores, its first production was a failure, and it was not performed again until after his death.

For years, Tchaikovsky had tried for success with an opera. This success had so far eluded him, but he now started work on an opera based on *Eugene Onegin*, a dramatic poem by Pushkin. The heroine, Tatiana, falls in love with Onegin, a cynical and restless character, and, in one scene, writes a letter declaring her love for him. The music so well interprets the tender and touching emotions of a young girl in love that Tchaikovsky himself was the first to be moved by it.

By an unfortunate coincidence, while working on this music, he received a letter from a young woman who, without encouragement from him, had fallen in love with him. In this letter, she threatened to kill herself if he did not return her love. Tchaikovsky, although never comfortable with women, nevertheless wanted someday to marry and have a family. Although he did not love her, he did not want to play in his own life a part like that played by Onegin in his opera, and he married the girl. As might seem evident from her letter alone, she was not too well balanced, and their marriage, from the honeymoon on, was disastrous for both of them.

Tchaikovsky was so miserable that he tried to drown himself in the river but succeeded only in catching pneumonia. His brother took him to Switzerland to recover, while his wife remained in Russia. They never lived together again, and the unfortunate woman spent her last years in a mental institution.

Tchaikovsky continued to compose. Thanks to Madame von Meck's financial support, he was able to travel. He had the mixed pleasure and pain of discovering that his music was valued more highly outside his native land than in it. At home in Russia he had been unhappy because he was not appreciated. Away from Russia, he was unhappy because he was homesick.

His music expressed not only his own loneliness and his yearning for peace and happiness, but the gloomy feelings of what became known as the "Russian soul." Evidently, many non-Russians shared these feelings, for Tchaikovsky's symphonies and other works were soon very popular. He became world renowned and was invited to conduct in the United States in 1891. By this time he had acquired enough poise to control his shyness and nervousness in public, and he was a good conductor. His fame brought him commissions for other operas and ballets. Even the czar took note of his success and granted him a pension.

In 1890 he received a strange letter from Madame von Meck, who told him that, as her own funds were running low, she was discontinuing his pension, and would no longer correspond with him. Although Tchaikovsky no longer needed her money so desperately, he could not understand why she wished to break off their friendship. When he learned that she had suffered no financial difficulties, and had lied to him, he was completely stunned. He had considered her his closest friend, and for fourteen years he had confided his most intimate thoughts to her.

He never recovered wholly from her abrupt destruction of their friendship, although the honors he received, including an honorary doctorate from Cambridge University, helped soften the blow to his feelings. To this day, Madame von Meck's reasons for breaking with Tchaikovsky are unknown.

In the summer of 1893 he returned to his home near Moscow, where he finished his most famous symphony, the Sixth, known as the *Pathétique*. A few months later he became ill, and he drank a glass of tap water. At that time tap water in Russia was known to be highly unsafe, and to drink it was either an act of foolishness or of suicide. Whatever his reasons, Tchaikovsky suffered the consequences, dying of cholera only a few days later, and his death started rumors that he had actually used this method to kill himself.

Sergei Vasilyevich Rachmaninoff
(1873–1943)

Sergei Rachmaninoff was born in 1873 to an upper-class Russian family that had lost its money. Encouraged to make a career in music, he graduated with honors from the Moscow Conservatory, where Tchaikovsky himself took a great interest in his talents as a composer. He was a magnificent pianist and a fine conductor, but his main interest was composition.

While still a student he had written a number of piano preludes, of which the one in C sharp minor was played so frequently that Rachmaninoff grew to hate it. Nevertheless, it made his name known both in Europe and in the United States and helped create an audience for his other compositions. These included four piano concertos, of which the second and third are extremely popular, several symphonies, operas, songs, and piano music.

Rachmaninoff was a tall, gaunt man with a sad and somber face that seemed to go well with his own music. His concertos, especially, are highly romantic and express the same melancholy longing for the past that can be found in the work of Tchaikovsky.

92. *Sergei Rachmaninoff.* (*Courtesy RCA Victor Records*)

The Russian Revolution of 1917 marked the end of the life he yearned for, and Rachmaninoff left Russia with his wife and children, eventually to settle in the United States. Here he continued to work until he died, still longing for a beloved Russia that no longer existed.

ITALY IN THE NINETEENTH CENTURY

For a long time Italian music seemed untouched by the romantic movement going on elsewhere. Opera was still the preferred form of musical art, and the human voice the best-loved instrument. Despite the fact that the Italian Renaissance had opened a new musical world, that the first piano had been constructed by an Italian, and that the violin family had been perfected by Italians, purely instrumental music did not thrive in Italy as it did elsewhere.

Among Italian composers of opera, Rossini was pre-eminent. But there were others of almost equal fame, like Vincenzo Bellini (1801–35), who wrote ten operas before his premature death, and Gaetano Donizetti (1797–1848), who wrote seventy. The poet Heinrich Heine said that Donizetti's speed in turning out operas was surpassed only by the speed of rabbits turning out new rabbits.

These men, however, did not write primarily for Italian opera houses. The average Roman or Venetian might have been a remarkably faithful operagoer, but he was poor, and his patronage did not make a composer rich. It did, however, give the composer a good reputation and helped him along on his way to Paris.

The Italian composer whose music not only remained Italian in melody and temperament, but was also addressed primarily to Italian audiences, was Giuseppe Verdi.

Giuseppe Verdi (1813–1901)

Born in the same year as Wagner, Verdi was the son of a poor innkeeper in the village of Roncole, which was under the rule of Napoleon. When Verdi was a year old, an Austrian army took the town, and his mother hid him in the church belfry. The invaders looted and killed at will, and the entire area was placed under Austrian rule. From infancy on, Verdi lived under the hated foreign oppressors, and the experience shaped his thoughts and, later on, his music.

When they learned that their son had talent, Verdi's parents somehow managed to pay for organ lessons, and even bought him a broken-down spinet. At the age of twelve, while still a schoolboy, he was appointed organist of the church.

So that Giuseppe might receive a better education than the village could offer, his parents sent him to school in Busseto, a nearby town. Here he attracted the interest of a well-to-do grocer, Antonio Barezzi. When Verdi completed his schooling, Barezzi gave him a part-time job, arranged for further musical training, and let him live in his own home, where Verdi enjoyed playing duets with Barezzi's pretty young daughter, Margherita.

When he was eighteen, Verdi sought admission to the conservatory in Milan. His application was rejected both because he was too old—most of the students were younger—and because the examination committee did not like the composition he wrote. Upset by the rejection, Verdi had to study privately. Through his teacher, Verdi met many prominent people and became familiar with many operas.

When Verdi was twenty, Barezzi offered him the vacant position of organist at the Busseto Cathedral. Verdi returned to Busseto partly because of the offer and partly to be near Margherita. Some of the townspeople objected to his appointment, and Verdi finally became organist at a rival church and conductor of the local *filarmonico,* or symphony orchestra. Two years later he married Margherita.

In 1839 he brought Margherita and their two children to Milan, where his opera *Oberto* had been accepted. But its production was delayed indefinitely, and it took the efforts of all Verdi's friends, and especially of Giuseppina Strepponi, a soprano in the company, to ensure its performance.

Although *Oberto* was only moderately successful, it was bought by a publisher, Giovanni Ricordi, now one of the great names in music publishing. Verdi signed a contract for three new operas in two years, but he disliked the librettos offered him, and for a year

93. *Giuseppe Verdi at the podium. From a painting. (New York Public Library)*

he was unable to get started. When he finally began work on an *opera buffa* he became ill, and as he was recovering, his wife and children sickened. Within a short time, they were all dead. Devastated by the tragedy, Verdi had to go ahead with the painful note-by-note composition of a farcical opera that died the night it was performed. The Milanese audience hissed, and Verdi never forgave them for it.

He now decided that he would never write another opera, but would support himself by teaching. However, the director of La Scala Opera Theater tracked him down, thrust a libretto upon him, and managed him so skillfully that Verdi settled down to compose *Nabucco*. The story dealt with the captivity of the ancient Hebrews in Babylon by Nabucco (Nebuchadnezzar). Produced in 1842, the opera was a sensational success, and not only because of its vigor and dramatic strength. The Italian audiences knew that a chorus of Hebrews lamenting their captivity expressed the feelings of Italians lamenting their own captivity under the Austrians. The words and music of the chorus swept through Italy.

The Austrian authorities decided that the liberation chorus was in fact a call for the overthrow of the Austrian government of occupation. They scrutinized the libretto of Verdi's next opera word for word and demanded a number of changes that Verdi refused to accept. In the end he compromised: he would change the words *Ave Maria* to *Salve Maria*.

Verdi now passed through a period in which almost every opera he wrote succeeded. The librettos were usually silly and called for the spilling of a great deal of blood, but Verdi was steadily increasing in skill as a composer, and his music made up for some of the weaknesses of the words and plots.

Always present to keep him on his toes were the censors. They objected to *Rigoletto*, based on a play by the French writer Victor Hugo, on the ground that the king in the opera was portrayed as a villain, and that innocent audiences might get the impression that all kings were villains. Verdi solved that problem by demoting the king and making him a mere duke. *A Masked Ball* dealt

94. *Verdi and his wife (seated at his right) in their garden with friends.*
(*G. Ricordi, Courtesy Franco Colombo, Inc.*)

with the murder of a king, and its performance was permitted only when the locale was changed to Massachusetts during the time of the Puritans, and the king was made a governor.

Verdi had for a number of years been living with Giuseppina Strepponi, the singer who had interceded in behalf of his first opera. They married in 1859, and the marriage proved to be a very happy one.

By now Verdi was world famous. His operas were performed in opera houses all over Europe, and he traveled a great deal, conducting his own works. He was also an active supporter of the cause of Italian independence, and his name, composed of the first letters of *Vittorio Emanuele, Re d'Italia* (*Victor Emanuel,*

King of Italy), became a national symbol. When Italy finally achieved independence, Verdi was elected to the first parliament. He disliked politics and politicians, but he served five years from a sense of duty.

In 1869 he received a request from the Khedive of Egypt for a new opera, to be performed in celebration of the opening of the Suez Canal. At first Verdi refused. But when he heard the libretto, he agreed to write the opera if his terms were met. He wanted 150,000 francs in gold for the Egyptian rights alone. He himself would retain all rights in other countries.

The Khedive agreed to Verdi's terms. However, the first performance had to be postponed because of the outbreak of the Franco-Prussian War. Verdi donated money to care for wounded French soldiers and, unlike Wagner, hoped that Paris would be spared destruction.

Aïda was finally presented in Cairo on Christmas Eve, 1871,

95. *Arrigo Boito, composer, and Verdi's librettist for* Otello *and* Falstaff. (*New York Public Library*)

and its tremendous success has continued to this day. Verdi himself did not attend. He disliked sea voyages.

In 1873 a famous writer, Manzoni, died, and Verdi wrote a *Requiem* in his memory. It is a beautiful work, almost operatic in some of its effects.

After the *Requiem,* Verdi rested. Thirteen years later, at seventy-three, he presented the world with *Otello,* a magnificent work based on Shakespeare's *Othello.* In 1893, his final opera, *Falstaff,* based on another Shakespearean character, amazed and delighted the world of music with its wit and comedy. In these last two operas he had a most talented librettist, Arrigo Boito (1842–1918), who was himself a composer. Boito knew that a libretto must also be a work of art, and he created taut, skillful scripts.

Verdi's wife died in 1897, and Verdi himself in 1901. He had lived a useful and creative life. Generous while still alive, he also left money to establish a home for old and sick musicians after his death. A peasant from Roncole, as he called himself, he was mourned as artist, patriot, philanthropist, and human being.

Giacomo Puccini (1858–1924)

Giacomo Puccini, who succeeded Verdi in the affections of Italian opera audiences, was, like Bach, a member of a family of musicians. His father, a church organist, died when Giacomo, one of seven children, was only six years old. Although the young boy was no prodigy, at fourteen he was helping to support the family by working as a church organist himself.

At twenty he attended a performance of *Aïda* and was stirred by its glamour and excitement. Opera, he decided, offered the kind of life he wanted to live.

He went to Milan to study at the same conservatory that had once rejected Verdi. He had better luck, for he was not only accepted, but had as his teacher Amilcare Ponchielli (1834–86), composer of the opera *La Gioconda.* Ponchielli encouraged him

96. Giacomo Puccini and his wife. (Courtesy Franco Colombo, Inc.)

to enter an operatic competition, and when Puccini failed to win, his teacher helped raise enough money to ensure the opera's production. *Le Villi* (*The Wilis,* or *Dancing Spirits*) was a great success, and a career as an operatic composer now lay wide open before him.

His next opera was a failure, and Puccini immediately went on to a third. *Manon Lescaut,* a novel by Abbé Prévost, had already inspired an opera, *Manon,* by Jules Massenet, but Puccini was fascinated by the opportunities the story gave him, and he wrote an opera quite different from that of Massenet. The first-night audience was moved to tears by the beauty of the music, and Puccini's *Manon Lescaut* soon appeared all over Italy, as well as in the rest of Europe. George Bernard Shaw hailed Puccini as the heir of Verdi.

Puccini believed in what the Italians called *"verismo,"* a kind of realism whose aim was to present realistic people in realistic emotional situations. Although he could also write a Chinese operatic fairy tale, such as his final work, *Turandot,* his music always expressed the way in which people in love, in anger, pain, or sorrow would feel.

In *La Bohème,* also based on a French novel, Puccini depicted the Parisian world of penniless young artists, musicians, and poets. This was a life he himself had known as a student in Milan. The tragic story of the doomed heroine and her lover retains its emotional power and is one of the best-loved operas.

Among the more famous of his other operas are *Madama Butterfly,* the tale of an unhappy love affair between a young Japanese girl and an American naval officer, and *Tosca,* a dramatic and often hair-raising story set in Rome at the time of Napoleon. *La Fanciulla del West,* usually known as *The Girl of the Golden West,* is an incredible Italian version of a very old-fashioned American Western melodrama, but it contains much effective music.

An attractive man, Puccini had trouble with a jealous wife, whose slanderous statements about her husband and their young servant girl caused the girl to commit suicide. His wife was sentenced to jail, but Puccini paid a large sum of money to keep her free.

Puccini's fame was world-wide, and he came to the United States in 1907 and 1910 for performances of his operas. A few years later he began to suffer from what was first considered a sore throat and was later diagnosed as cancer. Puccini underwent an operation, and although at first he seemed to be improving, the disease could not be controlled, and death came in 1924.

With Puccini's death, the attention of many Italian musicians turned away from opera to orchestral music. Even with the help of a subsidy from the Italian Government, it was becoming more and more expensive to produce new operas, and the odds against a composer attaining wealth and fame through operas became continually greater. What was true of Italy was even truer of the rest of the world. In the middle of the twentieth century, most composers sought recognition in other kinds of music.

CZECHOSLOVAKIA

The country we now call Czechoslovakia was born in 1918. For several centuries before that, it had been ruled by Austria, and its Slovakian, Bohemian, and Carpathian inhabitants had almost no rights. German was the official language, and the teaching of native languages was prohibited. Other manifestations of native culture were also discouraged, for the Austrian rulers knew only too well that a nation's pride in its own music, art, and literature was frequently accompanied by a desire for freedom.

The Bohemians, or Czechs, as they called themselves, had produced many fine musicians, and Prague, the principal city, had received the operas of Mozart far more enthusiastically than had Vienna. But the music that concert audiences heard was German, French, or Italian, never Czech.

Czech music was limited to folk songs until, in the nineteenth century, a new type of Czech music was created by Bedřich Smetana. Although it was based on folk music, Smetana's imagination wove the simple melodies that were part of Czech culture and tradition into works of a much more complicated art.

Bedřich Smetana (1824–84)

The son of a brewer, Smetana was raised in comfort. He played in quartets with his father when he was only six, and at eight made his debut as a pianist.

Music lover though he was, the elder Smetana opposed his son's musical ambitions, especially since the family had lost most of its income. The young man, however, found a teacher who was willing to give him lessons on credit for a time. On the point of starvation, Smetana later obtained a position as music teacher to a count. While traveling with his employer, he met Clara and Robert Schumann, as well as Franz Liszt. The symphonic poems of Liszt were to have a great influence on his musical thinking.

In 1848, the year of revolutions, he left the count's service, possibly because he had shown too much sympathy for the unsuccessful attempts to overthrow Austrian rule. The next year, with some aid from Liszt, he opened a music school in Prague. Several years of struggle to keep the school ended in failure, and Smetana, now married, accepted a flattering offer from Sweden. His wife died there in 1859, and Smetana remarried.

In 1861 he returned to his homeland. The Austrian army had been beaten in several battles in Italy, and the emperor thought it wise to make minor concessions to his other subjects. He therefore relaxed some of the rules against Czech culture, and a group of Czech patriots raised funds to build a theater where works by Czech artists could be performed. For the first time in his life, Smetana could write the kind of music he wanted, with reasonable assurance that it would be performed.

He applied his talent and skill to plots drawn from Czech history and legend. He wrote eight patriotic operas, all dealing in one way or another with the struggle for freedom and democracy. In 1866, his great comic opera *The Bartered Bride* was produced in Prague. At its first performance, this delightful work, which treats the peasants not as stupid brutes but as human beings,

97. *Bedřich Smetana.* (*Courtesy Czechoslovak Society of America*)

received only moderate applause. But its charming folk-like music, humor, and lively dances were so appealing that it caught on rapidly and became a favorite everywhere.

Smetana was honored now, and successful. He had suffered for years, however, from bad headaches, and in 1874 he suddenly became totally deaf. No longer able to conduct, he was retired on a small pension. His Swedish friends arranged for a medical examination by a famous specialist, who found that

Smetana's condition was hopeless. During this dreadful time Smetana, like Beethoven, wrote some of his most powerful works. A quartet, subtitled *From My Life,* expresses his vitality and love of life despite the tragedy of his deafness. And his symphonic cycle of six tone poems, entitled *My Country,* paints in beautiful sound his pride in his homeland.

But the end was approaching. Smetana began to suffer from profound mental depression, he heard noises in his head, and both his speech and his memory were soon affected. He died a month after admission to an asylum.

Smetana is honored as the founder of Czech music, and the Smetana Museum in Prague commemorates the life and work of a man who loved his own country without hating the countries of other men.

Antonin Dvořák (1841–1904)

When Antonin Dvořák was born, it was assumed that he would become, like his father, a butcher and innkeeper and perhaps make a slightly better income than most of his family of poor peasants. He learned how to play the violin as a child and would entertain the patrons at the inn with his renditions of folk songs. He also took music lessons from the choirmaster of the local church.

At fourteen, he was apprenticed to a butcher, but with music on his mind Antonin did not make a very good apprentice, and when he was about sixteen, his parents finally sent him to the organ school in Prague.

He was not very happy there. His schoolmates laughed at this stocky young peasant's bad pronunciation of German and at his idea of becoming a composer. But the young peasant was in earnest. To support himself, he played the violin or piano in cafés and theaters and the organ in a church.

In addition, he composed. As he usually did this late at night, when his other work was done, and often tried out his

98. Antonin Dvořák. (Courtesy Czechoslovak Society of America)

ideas at the piano, he became an unpopular boarder and was frequently evicted from his lodgings.

His first professional success came when he was over thirty, with the performance of a patriotic cantata. The poem to which he had set the music dealt with the Austrian oppression of the Czechs, and the cantata aroused an enthusiastic response from his audiences. In the same year, he married. Like Haydn and

Mozart, Dvořák had first fallen in love with a sister of the girl he eventually married. Unlike Haydn and Mozart, he had a happy marriage.

In 1874 Dvořák became organist in a large church and was also given a musical grant by the government. His income from both sources, together with the fees from a few pupils, was barely enough to support a wife and child. Fortunately for Dvořák, one of the judges on the awards committee was Johannes Brahms, who was impressed with his work. Brahms found him a publisher, and from that moment on, Dvořák's life became a success story, his compositions being well received by the public, both in performance and in publication.

He had steeped himself so thoroughly in the folk music of his country that many listeners are surprised to learn that the melodies in such compositions as the *Slavonic Dances* are not folk songs or dances at all, but are original with Dvořák. The same folk quality can be found in all his music, from operas, symphonies, and concertos to chamber music and pieces for the piano.

In 1892 he was invited to direct a conservatory in New York City. He enjoyed his stay in the United States and went sightseeing in many parts of the country. Among the places he visited with particular pleasure was a Bohemian farm colony in Iowa.

He was fascinated by the American folk songs and Negro spirituals he heard, and he felt that both, especially the Negro songs, could become the foundation of a new kind of American music, "the voice of a free and great nation." His own symphony *From the New World* shows how he himself was able to use such musical inspiration.

He always retained a great warmth of feeling for the people of the New World, and later he made another trip here. Meanwhile at the Prague Conservatory, he had acquired a reputation as a very strict and demanding teacher who commanded both the attention and devotion of his pupils. One of his students, Joseph Suk (1874–1935), who was also to become a well-known composer, married Dvořák's daughter.

Dvořák received honors from many countries, including a doctorate from Cambridge University. He died of a heart attack in 1904.

French Impressionists

Throughout the rule of Napoleon and of the various kings and presidents that followed each other across the French political stage, grand opera, accompanied by ballet, continued to be the craze in Paris.

Strangely enough, it was the foreigners who best wrote opera to the satisfaction of French audiences. A native Frenchman like Berlioz tried it and failed, but Rossini, Bellini, and Meyerbeer drew audiences in droves.

Among the most successful composers of lighter works was the German-born Jacques Offenbach (1819–80), who wrote witty, sophisticated operettas that often dealt with the ancient Greek myths. His tongue-in-cheek versions of *Orpheus in the Underworld,* and of *Beautiful Helen* (*Helen of Troy*) were very unlike the original stories. His one serious opera, the fantastic *Tales of Hoffmann,* was not produced until after his death.

In the middle of the nineteenth century, art, literature, and music became more naturalistic. Painters, writers, and composers tried to show life as it was and people as they really behaved, even if the behavior and the life were ugly. In opera, of course, the idea of showing people as they were was limited by the conventions of opera itself. In real life, people do not break into song to express their feelings toward each other, nor do they have an orchestra to follow them around ready to accompany arias and duets.

The most famous naturalistic opera was *Carmen,* by Bizet. A girl who worked in a cigarette factory, Carmen was a far cry from the noble heroines of history and mythology.

Georges Bizet (*1838–75*)

At the age of nine, Georges Bizet was already a conservatory student, and before he was twenty he won the *Prix de Rome*. He wrote charming piano and symphonic music, and several operas, of which *Carmen* is the most famous.

Bizet's heroine not only worked for a living. She was also a smuggler and, as heroines then went, not very moral. The hero of the opera, Don José, was a soldier who deserted the army for love of her, himself became a smuggler, and finally killed her in a jealous rage.

Fifty years before, a plot like this would have made a composer shudder. For Bizet, it offered the opportunity to write a dramatic masterpiece. His music has a wealth of melody, and it makes such exciting use of Spanish-inspired rhythms that the sordid yet tragic tale is spellbinding.

The audience that attended *Carmen's* premiere was both repelled and fascinated. Bizet, who had been ill with heart disease for some time, died soon after, and it was said that disappointment over the reception of the opera had hastened his death. If he had lived just a few years longer, he would have seen *Carmen* become one of the most popular operas of all time.

Among the other composers who wrote operas and contributed to the development of symphonic literature was Camille Saint-Saëns (1835–1921). Saint-Saëns is said to have been the first Frenchman to write a symphonic poem. He was a masterful orchestrator who composed fluently for stage, orchestra, and solo instruments. His opera *Samson and Delilah* is performed frequently, and his *Carnival of Animals* has delighted concert audiences, both young and old, for generations.

César Franck (1822–90) was born in Belgium but settled in Paris as a young man. He was extremely devout and, as a church organist, composed a number of religious works. He did not re-

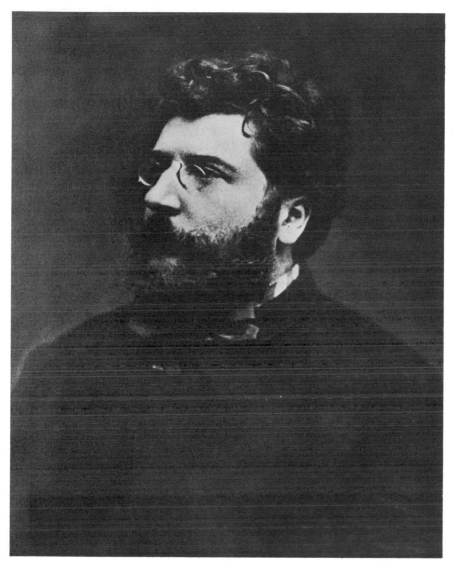

99. Georges Bizet. (Courtesy French Cultural Services)

ceive recognition for his symphonic and chamber works until he was about sixty, but he was always cheerful and pleasant in disposition. He taught at the conservatory and had a great influence on a number of French musicians. His only symphony, a very romantic piece of music, is a great favorite with audiences.

100. A scene from an early production of Carmen. *Photo by Pic.* (*Courtesy Paris Opera Museum*)

In 1863, Claude Monet, an artist, exhibited a painting that was to have a considerable influence on French music. Monet called his work *Sunrise—Impression.* In it, Monet had turned away from detailed realism and had painted his impression of a sunrise. Monet was only the first of a famous group of artists who attempted to use light, shade, and color to create a mood.

In its rivalry with naturalism, impressionism was aided by the improvements in photography. A photographer could produce a scene more detailed and more accurate than any painter could, and in much less time. The painter who considered himself an artist had no desire to compete with the camera. If he was inferior to the photographer in this respect, however, he was superior in many other ways, and he could do what the camera could not. He could disregard the petty details and convey what he considered more important—the atmosphere and moods of real life.

From painting, the trend toward impressionism spread to the other arts. Poets and dramatists too began to emphasize their ability to create mood and atmosphere, instead of attempting to describe a scene or action in great detail.

It was not long before composers also joined the impressionist movement. In their creation of mood and atmosphere, no longer would they limit themselves to reproducing in their music such effects as the call of the cuckoo or other birds, or the sounds of rain and thunderstorms.

Claude Achille Debussy (*1862–1918*)

Claude Debussy was born to a poor shopkeeper the year before Monet's *Sunrise* was exhibited. He showed his talent at so early an age that his father, who had planned a naval career for him, resigned himself to Claude's becoming a musician. When he realized that a prodigy could make a fortune, he even forced the boy to practice.

Claude's father was destined for disappointment, for Claude never became a concert pianist. His gift lay not in performance but in his musical imagination. By the time he was eleven, he was studying at the conservatory. His teachers appreciated his talents sufficiently to recommend him, at seventeen, to Madame von Meck, Tchaikovsky's patroness, as a pianist and music teacher for her children. He spent three summers with the Von Meck family, visiting Russia, Italy, and Switzerland and had the opportunity to hear the music of Russian and Italian composers in their native lands. He also enjoyed the luxurious life of the upper classes.

In 1884, on his third attempt, he won the *Prix de Rome,* shrewdly fitting the composition he submitted to the tastes of the judges. His victory was a hollow one, for it turned out that he hated Rome. At this time he was an ardent Wagnerite, and it was not until several years later, after he had returned to Paris, that he became critical of his idol's music.

When he was twenty-seven, he sat through the four evenings needed for a complete performance of Wagner's *Ring of the Nibelungs.* As the music drama went on and on, he was not only bored but repelled by what seemed to him an overblown orchestra and overlong repetitions of the same themes. He left the opera house on the fourth night just as ardently opposed to Wagner as he had previously been for him.

With no foreign idol to worship, he began to think seriously of his role as a composer and a Frenchman. Debussy had more than his share of French nationalism, and he felt that his music must be an expression of the French personality.

The French personality, as he saw it, possessed clarity, elegance, and delicacy of taste. The music he would create for it would therefore not be based on folk melodies, which he thought crude and far from delicate, but would be to the ear what the paintings of Monet and the other impressionist artists were to the eye. Debussy was attracted to the exotic instruments and tones of Oriental music, and he believed that such sounds would heighten the effects of his own compositions. He hoped that his impressionist music would put an end to the influence, in France, of what he considered the heavy-handed sentimentality of the German composers.

But French audiences could not easily grasp Debussy's impressions of the French personality. And at a concert where some of his works were performed, a quartet he had written confused not only the audience but the musicians who played it.

Gradually, however, Debussy's ideas and music won acceptance. Audiences began to appreciate his skillful use of the orchestra, of the piano, and of the human voice. Yet the same old doubts arose upon the production of his opera, *Pelléas and Mélisande.* This broke completely with operatic traditions, and critics questioned whether it was an opera at all. The text, based on the play of the same name by Maurice Maeterlinck, was obscure and confusing, the setting had a dreamlike quality, and the action, if it could be called that, was shrouded in mystery, so that the audience could never be sure what was supposed to be reality and what unreality.

The opera became, and still remains, the subject of controversy. Its admirers called it a masterpiece, while its detractors denounced it as pretentious and dull.

Debussy's most famous orchestral composition, *Prelude to the*

101. Claude Debussy around 1894. (Courtesy French Cultural Services)

Afternoon of a Faun, inspired by a poem of Stéphane Mal-
larmé, was first presented as a ballet. In this music Debussy
evokes a mood of shimmering heat and sensuous dreams.

Debussy had lived a rather bohemian existence in Montmartre,
the section of Paris where artists congregated, until, in 1899, he
married for the first time. When he left his wife for another
woman, his wife tried to kill herself. The fact that his wife was
poor and the other woman wealthy helped turn the public against
him. Although his unheroic role in the separation and divorce
alienated many of his friends, his second marriage was a happy
one, and he had a child for whom he wrote charming piano pieces.

By now he was world famous, and the impressionism he championed had won the respect of musicians all over the world.
Nevertheless, his compositions were still attacked by other musicians and by critics, as well as by the clergy. The Archbishop of
Paris condemned his choral ballet, *The Martyrdom of St. Sebastian,* and threatened with excommunication any Catholic who
attended a performance. Later it was performed successfully, even
in Rome.

Debussy was interested in the work of other composers, and
at the beginning of the twentieth century he had warm words for
the compositions of a young Frenchman named Ravel. Their friendship soured, however, when it became clear that the younger
man was a rival to be taken seriously.

Debussy was in poor health when World War I began, and
he suffered deeply during the early days of the war, when his
beloved France was invaded and appeared to face disaster. He
lived until March 1918, however, long enough to see the tide turn
against the invading Germans.

Maurice Ravel (1875–1937)

Born in the Basque region of France, near the Spanish border,
Maurice Ravel was encouraged by his father to become a musician. At fourteen, he entered the Paris Conservatory, and at

twenty-two he studied composition with Gabriel Fauré (1845–1924). Fauré was a church organist and the composer of many interesting works. As a teacher, he had two great and unusual virtues: he encouraged his students to think for themselves musically, and he treated them as his equals.

Ravel was a composer of sensuous, romantic, and colorful music, and his work was influenced by the music of Spain, Russia, and the Far East. Audiences found it difficult to become accustomed to his exotic sounds, and his first orchestral composition, performed in 1899, was greeted with hisses. During the next few years Ravel's reputation grew, but it brought him little money to live on, and in 1901 he entered the contest for the *Prix de Rome*. He won only the second prize.

Ravel tried again, making in all four attempts to win the prize. On his last try, in 1905, he ended up worse than he had done on his first. Many musicians regarded his failure to win as evidence of the insulting stupidity of the judges, and they created such a furor that some of the excessively conservative directors of the conservatory were replaced.

Ravel shrugged off his failure to win the prize and went on with his work. His opera, *L'Heure espagnole* (*The Spanish Hour*), was a sophisticated comedy of love, marriage, and clocks, but was not performed until 1911, as the opera managers feared that it might be considered indecent. It is now given, without shocking anyone, in commercial opera houses and is a favorite in college opera productions.

Rhapsodie espagnole, another composition inspired by his feeling for Spanish music, was both cheered and hissed at its first performance. As the uproar created by friends and foes made it impossible to hear the music, it was repeated and became a success. *Daphnis and Chloé*, a ballet based on an ancient Greek myth, was a failure, but Ravel's music so effectively created a romantic atmosphere for the archaic tale that it became a popular concert piece.

By this time Ravel was well known, and he and Debussy were regarded as the two leading impressionist composers.

102. *Maurice Ravel. (Courtesy French Cultural Services)*

Ravel was a short man, only five feet tall, and was vain about his appearance. He dressed elegantly and spent so much time choosing exactly the right shade of gloves or shirt to wear that he was almost always late for appointments. Friends would wait for him, but trains would not, and he missed almost as many as he caught.

Although Ravel never married, he was very fond of children, and would play with them and their toys for hours. He himself collected all sorts of mechanical toys.

When World War I started he tried several times to enlist in the French army and was rejected. He finally managed to be accepted as a front-line truck driver. He was eventually discharged from the army for medical reasons, and it took him a long time to regain his health.

Despite his desire to see France and her allies win the war, Ravel did not carry his enmity to Germany over into music. He denounced those chauvinistic Frenchmen who tried to prevent the performance of music by composers whose countries were at war with France. A patriot himself, he did not regard it as unpatriotic to play the music of Bach, Haydn, Mozart, Beethoven, and Schubert.

In 1920 he was offered the award of the French Legion of Honor and created an uproar by refusing it. He could not forget the official slap in the face when he had so consistently and so insultingly been refused the *Prix de Rome*. Besides, he said, he doubted any government's ability to recognize talent.

In 1927 he toured the United States, made a great deal of money by giving concerts, and was fascinated by American jazz. Some of the music he wrote on his return to France shows a jazz influence. But he still retained his love for Spanish music, and his most famous orchestral composition was inspired by a Spanish dance, the bolero. Ravel's *Bolero* was composed for a famous dancer, and it consists of a single melody, played with an insistent rhythm, and repeated again and again, growing louder and using more instruments at each repetition. The first performance created a sensation.

In 1933 he became ill with what was eventually diagnosed as a brain tumor. In 1937, despite short periods of improvement, his condition was so desperate that he was operated on. He died a week after the operation, without recovering consciousness.

Erik Satie and The Six

One of the musicians whose ideas had considerable influence on Ravel's early compositions was Erik Satie (1866–1925), who had also been a good friend of Debussy. Satie himself composed a great deal, but publishers and performers showed only slight interest in his work, and, to support himself, he became for a time pianist in a night club. His compositions were witty and ironic but could not compete with the sensuous music of Debussy and Ravel. Satie was criticized for writing music that had no form, and he replied to what he considered an idiotic accusation by giving some of his pieces such titles as *Three Pieces in the Form of a Pear.*

Relatively unsuccessful as a composer, Satie was alert to what was happening in the different arts, and was able to recognize and encourage new trends in musical composition. Long before Ravel's death, painters and writers had moved away from impressionism, which they regarded as old-fashioned. New and bewildering movements appeared under the names of cubism, dadaism, surrealism.

Satie helped obtain a hearing for a group of composers who called themselves "The Six," the members including Darius Milhaud (1892–   ), Francis Poulenc (1899–1965), Arthur Honegger (1892–1955), Georges Auric (1899–   ), Louis Durey (1888–   ), and Germaine Tailleferre (1892–   ), that rarity among composers, a woman.

The Six regarded their music as a reflection of the modern world, and their cynical, discordant compositions attracted musicians from all over Europe and the United States. Milhaud, Poulenc, Honegger, and Auric achieved international recognition, but their music no longer evoked the hisses it once did. A new generation of composers condemns it as too respectable and conservative.

SPAIN

Spain is a country in which many different strains of people have lived. The Greeks, the Romans, the Visigoths, and the Moors have all contributed to Spanish culture in general, while the Catalans and the Basques have to a large extent retained their own languages and cultures.

As the result of the long occupation of Spain by the Moors, from the eighth century to the end of the fifteenth, Spanish music and dance show a strong Oriental influence. They have always fascinated musicians of all nations. Composers have borrowed the rhythms of the fandango, bolero, habanera, and other dances, but Spanish musicians themselves have not, until recently, occupied a prominent place in the musical world.

For a long time the most highly regarded music in Spain was church music, for performance by chorus and organ. The courts had their troubadours and madrigal singers, who frequently accompanied their singing with the vihuela, a complicated Spanish type of lute. The vihuela was gradually replaced by the guitar, which was played by peasants and villagers and was found to be most effective in reproducing the distinctive Spanish folk rhythms. By the seventeenth century, the guitar had become the national instrument of Spain.

In the eighteenth century, King Philip V and his Italian-born wife invited Italian musicians and singers to Madrid. Among the best known of the visiting composers was Domenico Scarlatti, who had several Spanish students. One of them, Padre Antonio Soler, like his teacher, wrote many harpsichord sonatas.

Another gifted Italian who spent many years in Spain was Luigi Boccherini (1743–1805), who became so fond of the guitar that he wrote a number of chamber works for guitar and stringed instruments.

A young Basque musician, Juan Crisistomo de Arriaga (1806–

103. Lute-playing minstrels of thirteenth-century Spain. (New York Public Library)

26), might have breathed new life into Spanish concert music. Composer of a successful opera at the age of thirteen, he was sent to Paris to study, but died, unfortunately, before he was twenty-one.

It was not till near the end of the nineteenth century that a group of Spanish nationalist composers arose, who used the folk songs and dances of the various regions of Spain as the basis of their own art.

Isaac Albéniz (*1860–1909*)

Most of the life of Albéniz can best be described as unbelievable. The more believable part lasted for nine years. At the age of four he gave a piano recital and did so well that his father dreamed of the child's making the family fortune. At six, therefore, he was sent to Paris to study music. Life in Paris, however, seemed to this precocious youngster to be tame, and at nine he ran away to seek the kind of adventure he had read about in books.

He found it. He toured all of Spain, made money by playing the piano, and lost it all to a highway robber. He managed to reach Cádiz, where the governor was outraged at the thought of a child acting with greater independence and with more intelligence than the average adult, and he determined to return him to his father. Albéniz prevented this by stowing away on a ship bound for Puerto Rico.

He was discovered aboard ship and, as he had no money, was put ashore at Buenos Aires. Here he gave concerts so successfully that by the age of thirteen, when he reached Cuba, he had already earned a fortune, and he spent it almost as fast as he earned it. At this point his father gave up trying to make him return home.

After five more years of adventure, he returned to Europe for a more serious study of music. He became a student of Liszt and at twenty went touring again, this time as a finished concert pianist. He later studied with a Spanish composer, Felipe Pedrell (1841–1922), and gave up the concert stage to concentrate on composing.

His travels as a child and young man had put an end to his restlessness. He married, moved to Paris, and settled down to work. Despite the influence of French composers, all of his compositions have a unique Spanish flavor. His masterpiece is *Iberia*, the ancient name for the peninsula that includes Spain and Portu-

104. Isaac Albéniz. (New York Public Library)

gal. *Iberia* is a suite for piano that pictures the life and activities of the different parts of Spain—the languorous and the lively, the sad and the happy. It includes the music of Andalusia, Seville, Almería, and other areas.

Albéniz died at the age of forty-nine. Perhaps the adventure and adversity of his early life had weakened his health. In terms of activity, however, he had lived a century.

Enrique Granados (1867–1916)

In most respects, the life of Granados was very different from that of Albéniz. After studying music in Paris, he returned to Spain to teach music and to compose. Like Albéniz, he studied with Felipe Pedrell and was inspired to express in music the life of his country. He wrote many Spanish dances and other compositions. A great admirer of the painter Goya, he composed a suite, *Goyescas*, based on a group of drawings that Goya had made of Spanish life.

Later he turned the suite into an opera, which was performed at the Metropolitan Opera House in New York during World War I. Granados, who had always lived a quiet life at home, braved a sea voyage across the Atlantic Ocean to attend the first performance. On the return journey he and his wife both perished when their ship was torpedoed by a German submarine.

Manuel de Falla (1876–1946)

Outstanding among Spanish composers, Manuel de Falla lived in Spain till he was about thirty, and then settled in Paris for seven years, to study and to compose. Influenced by the French impressionist composers, he wrote much orchestral music in which he used the technical ability that he acquired in Paris to express Spanish inspirations and emotions.

While in Paris, he wrote the music for several ballets. *The Three-Cornered Hat* was produced by the Diaghilev Ballet in 1919, with sets and costumes by the famous Spanish painter Pablo Picasso. The ballet's lively and witty picture in music of Spanish peasants, its dance rhythms, and its skillful use of instruments make it highly popular in concert form.

The other ballet for which De Falla is known is *El Amor Brujo*, or *Love the Magician*. The plot is based on a gypsy legend, and its exciting music is inspired by the gypsy folk music called "flamenco."

De Falla also wrote several operas, one of them based on an episode from *Don Quixote* and intended for performance by puppets, with the singers offstage.

When the Spanish Civil War broke out in 1936, De Falla was not involved in either war or politics, and he stayed in Spain until 1939. That year, however, he left for Argentina, where he died.

SCANDINAVIA

For many centuries Denmark, Norway, Sweden, and Finland had little to do with the making of musical history.

English, Flemish, Italian, and German composers were invited to serve as directors of music in several of the Scandinavian courts, and their work was admired and imitated. But they left no particularly notable Scandinavian pupils or disciples. In the early seventeenth century, King Christian IV of Denmark sent groups of young musicians to study in London and Venice, but they too appear to have had little influence on the development of a native Scandinavian music.

The first Scandinavian composer to acquire a European reputation was Niels Vilhelm Gade (1817–90), but he was overshadowed by his contemporaries. Nowadays his works are seldom heard.

Edvard Hagerup Grieg (1843–1907)

Edvard Grieg, the great-grandson of a Scottish exile, was born in Bergen, Norway. His parents encouraged his interest in music, and he grew up familiar with the work of the famous composers.

At the age of fifteen Grieg met the famous Norwegian violinist Ole Bull, who was devoting his life to spreading knowledge of Norwegian folk songs. Bull brought this hitherto neglected music to Grieg's attention. Grieg had never suspected what a wealth of

105. Edvard Grieg. (Courtesy Norwegian Information Service)

melody could exist in folk music, and he became a convert to the cause. At the same time, Bull was impressed by Grieg's talent and suggested that he study in Germany. Grieg enrolled in the Leipzig Conservatory but was somewhat disappointed there. The teaching helped make him a fine pianist, but he always felt that the instruction in composition and orchestration was of low quality.

When he returned home, in 1862, he gave a concert of his

own works and applied for a government subsidy to continue his studies. The subsidy was not granted, and Grieg left for Copenhagen, which was more alive musically than any city in Norway.

In Copenhagen he met Rikard Nordraak (1842–66) who had composed the Norwegian National Anthem and was trying to develop a national Norwegian music. He and Grieg started a musical society for the performance of music by Scandinavian composers.

In 1866 Grieg returned to Norway, and the following year, against the opposition of his own family as well as his bride's, he married his cousin. She was a talented singer, and Grieg wrote many songs for her.

By this time Grieg's reputation was growing, but he was still without honor in his own country. To support his family, he had to take time from his composition to concentrate on teaching. He passed through a period of discouragement, when, quite unexpectedly, he received a warm and appreciative letter from the fabulous Franz Liszt, who was then in Rome.

The receipt of Liszt's letter was the turning point of his career. On the strength of it, he obtained a subsidy that in 1870 made it possible for him to visit Rome and to thank Liszt in person. Liszt was the first to hail Grieg's Piano Concerto, one of the most popular concertos ever written.

Grieg composed many lovely songs, much chamber music, and several orchestral suites, the best-known probably being the *Peer Gynt Suite*. The suite was written to accompany *Peer Gynt,* a dramatic fantasy by the Norwegian Henrik Ibsen, and the music very successfully captures the quality of the play.

Grieg was an ardent patriot and actively supported the cause of Norwegian freedom. For centuries Norway had been, in effect, a province of Denmark. In 1814, however, Denmark, which had allied itself with Napoleon, went down to defeat with the French emperor and was forced to yield Norway to Sweden. In 1905, after almost an entire century of struggle, Norway, to Grieg's joy, finally won complete independence.

Grieg died in 1907 after several years of illness.

Jean Sibelius (1865–1957)

Finland is a small country that has undergone centuries of foreign rule, first by Sweden, and later by Russia. Both powers discouraged native Finnish culture. As Finland had no independent ruler or court of its own, foreign musicians had little occasion to visit it, and until the nineteenth century many Finns were unaware that any form of music existed other than their own folk songs.

By the time of Jean Sibelius, however, a conservatory for the teaching of music had been founded in Helsinki, the capital of Finland. Sibelius studied here and showed such talent that the government gave him a grant to study first in Berlin and then in Vienna.

In the 1890s Finland was fighting for freedom from the Russian Government, and Sibelius took part in the struggle chiefly by means of his music. He immersed himself in Finnish folklore and history and was inspired to write a number of tone poems based on episodes from the epic *Kalevala*.

The music of Sibelius became a rallying point for his fellow Finns. In 1897, the Finnish Senate, despite the fact that it was under Russian domination, voted him a pension of two thousand marks a year. Sibelius used the money to support himself while he composed music. The tone poem *Finlandia* excited its listeners so greatly that the Russian Government prohibited public performances. The Finns evaded this prohibition by performing *Finlandia* under different names in different places.

The music of Sibelius expresses the somber, austere beauty of his homeland. Living in a luxurious log cabin not far from Helsinki, Sibelius for many years enjoyed comparative isolation. In his youth he had been attracted to the music of Grieg and Tchaikovsky, but as he grew older he tried to avoid the influences of other composers and rarely listened to anyone else's music.

Critics have differed violently in their evaluation of his music.

106. *Jean Sibelius and his wife. (Courtesy Finnish Information Service)*

Some have ranked him almost with Beethoven, while others have written him off as old-fashioned and out of touch with modern music. In Finland, of course, his greatness is taken for granted, and outside of Finland his violin concerto, his tone poems, and several of his symphonies are frequently played.

Béla Bartók (1881–1945)

Haydn, Schubert, Liszt, and Brahms all wove popular Hungarian folk melodies into their music. But they did not know these melodies as the peasants who were uninfluenced by city life sang them, and by the time the melodies reached concert audiences, they had lost much of their authentic Hungarian flavor. In the early years of the twentieth century, therefore, two Hungarian composers, Béla Bartók and Zoltán Kodály (1882–   ), started a serious study of their country's folk music by going into isolated communities and recording the words and music actually sung by the peasants.

Bartók and Kodály did not limit themselves to the peasants who spoke Hungarian. For purposes of comparison they also recorded the songs of the Slovak- and Rumanian-speaking peasants.

The more than six thousand folk tunes that the two young men collected were quite different from the tunes that Haydn and other composers had considered Hungarian. Most of them sounded strange to the ears of Bartók and Kodály, who realized that they were based on ancient scales or modes. Some of them had lost their strangeness when they had been picked up by gypsy musicians and rearranged for café audiences. Other folk tunes first thought to be authentically Hungarian turned out to be Slovak or Rumanian.

Bartók's interest in folk music began in childhood. Born in Hungary, he first took piano lessons from his mother at the age of seven. When his father died, his mother had to teach school in order to support the family, but he continued his lessons with more advanced teachers and made a public appearance as a pianist at the age of nine.

Almost always in poor health, Bartók worked hard to become a pianist and composer, and his first symphony was performed before an appreciative audience in 1904. His early compositions, strongly influenced by the work of Brahms, Liszt, and Wagner,

107. *Béla Bartók, center, rehearsing with Joseph Szigeti, violinist, and Benny Goodman, clarinetist. (Courtesy Columbia Records)*

were so highly regarded that when he was only twenty-six he became a professor of music at the Budapest Conservatory.

By this time, however, he had already begun to compose in a less popular manner. Strongly impressed by the power of the genuinely Hungarian melodies, he began to use their melodic lines and their abrupt and unconventional changes in rhythm in his own compositions. The strange melodies required equally strange harmonies to go along with them, and the resulting dissonances shocked the musicians and audiences of that day. The influence of the ancient folk melodies on Bartók's own compositions made his work sound extremely modern, so modern, in fact, that for a number of years no musical groups wanted to play them.

In 1940, after almost thirty years at the conservatory, he fled before advancing nazism to the United States, cutting himself off from both his pension and whatever royalties his compositions would have brought him. During the war years he lived and worked in poverty until his death, in New York, of leukemia. Since his death, his reputation has grown tremendously, and he is now regarded as one of the masters of modern music.

ENGLAND AGAIN

England, for centuries a warm and generous host to foreign musical visitors, has been less generous to her native composers.

Purcell's struggle to keep material body and musical soul together started a tradition. After him, other serious composers were so discouraged by their reception that they turned to some other ways of earning a living. Some abandoned music entirely; others became teachers, performers, or composers of operettas and theater music.

The most prominent English composer of the nineteenth century is probably Arthur Sullivan (1842–1900). To the witty and sparkling librettos of William S. Gilbert (1836–1911), Sullivan wrote music that captivated English audiences, as well as the American audiences who saw and heard pirated versions of the operettas in the United States. The combination of fame and financial success that his work achieved made Sir Arthur Sullivan, as he became, an unhappy man. Till the day of his death, he was embittered by the realization that the tuneful and unpretentious music he turned out for one operetta after another pleased millions of people, while the serious music he wrote with great effort apparently pleased no one, especially the critics.

Among the composers who fought doggedly to write serious music was Edward Elgar (1857–1934). Elgar's father was a musician and music salesman, and Elgar himself worked at many jobs, including that of music teacher at an insane asylum. Elgar had to fight the snobbishness of his audiences, and did so, eventually attaining knighthood and the title of Sir Edward Elgar.

Another composer, Frederick Delius (1862–1934) was born in England of German parentage. Inspired by Debussy and encouraged by Grieg, Delius composed music that used the technique of Debussy's impressionism and the material of English folk songs and dances to give the flavor of the English countryside. This feat is all the more remarkable, as Delius spent most of his life away from England. He lived for a time in Florida, where he grew oranges, and then in France, where he eventually died, paralyzed and blind.

The outstanding English national composer of this era is Ralph Vaughan Williams (1872–1958). Vaughan Williams became interested in English folk music as a young man, and this interest influenced his entire approach to composition. During World War I, he enlisted in the army as a private and learned what the ordinary Briton was like. He encouraged interest in folk music and folk festivals, as well as in the heritage of music from Elizabethan times.

Elgar, Delius, and Vaughan Williams helped create a minor renaissance in the music of their nation, and they reminded English composers that they had inherited a form of musical speech that could serve as musical raw material as well as the folk music of any other country. In our own time, such composers as Sir William Walton (1902–   ) and Benjamin Britten (1913–   ) have achieved international reputations. Britten is especially well known for his operas and for his *War Requiem,* which is a powerful and touching work.

X

COMPOSERS IN THE NEW WORLD

Music in the New World developed quite differently from that in Europe. The colonies in the Western Hemisphere were, for a long time, sparsely populated, and there was no wealthy nobility to import professional musicians from the Old World, more than three thousand miles away. Nor were there the large cities and theaters needed to attract a concertgoing public.

Some of the early settlers had been familiar with the best music of Europe and had even brought their musical instruments with them. But for a long time the condition of life in the New World made farmers and mechanics more valuable than musicians, and although professional musicians and teachers of music did exist, their numbers were small.

It was the day of the amateur musician. The colonists had brought folk music with them from their homelands, and this arrived in the New World not on music paper but in their minds and memories, where both words and music usually underwent many changes from the original. Families sang at home, and young people danced, often to the playing of a local fiddler and the rhythmic clapping of hands. In their more solemn moods, the colonists sang hymns in church.

As the colonies grew in population, the number of musicians and the interest in music also increased. Thomas Jefferson, for example, spent considerable time practicing the violin and playing in string quartets, while Benjamin Franklin invented the system of musical glasses, known as the armonica, for which Gluck and Mozart composed.

108. *A dance of the sort that took place in colonial America. Note the musicians on the platform. (Courtesy Library of Congress)*

While the old transplanted European folk songs continued to flourish, and new ones were created in the same style, an entirely different kind of folk music slowly developed in the American South. The thousands of slaves who had been brought from Africa created work songs, blues, freedom songs, and spirituals, many of them showing the influence of the original African rhythms. After the Civil War, when more Negroes moved to the cities, the musicians among them found work in cafés, restaurants, and dance halls, where their music was gradually transformed into a new kind of music called jazz.

Through most of the nineteenth century the music of the great European composers remained completely unknown to most Americans, although several symphony orchestras and traveling opera companies were active. The farmers and mountaineers who created and sang folk songs had never heard of Haydn or Beethoven, while the few people who did know the names and recognized a few compositions by these composers snobbishly turned up their noses at the folk music that surrounded them. The separation of the two kinds of music was made sharper by the fact that only the well-to-do could afford to attend concerts of serious music. During the latter part of the century it became customary for newly rich men to sponsor music—at first orchestral, and later operatic—which most of them could neither understand nor enjoy.

In this respect they differed little from the average member of the growing middle class, who also lacked a musical background. To attract people like these to serious music, the music had to be made less serious, and success came not to the best musician but to the most sensational performer. One pianist lured the audiences to see him by promising to play four hundred notes in a single measure. Not to be outdone, a singer boasted that he could sing six hundred words and three hundred measures in four minutes. Another pianist specialized in striking the keys, not merely with his fingers, but with his fists and elbows as well.

Serious American composers were isolated and unknown in their own country. Louis Moreau Gottschalk (1829–69) had to win recognition as a pianist in Paris before he could interest American audiences, and then it was as "the American Chopin." Edward MacDowell (1861–1908), born in New York City, had to go to France and Germany to advance his musical education. MacDowell adapted Indian melodies for use in his compositions, some of which are still played. MacDowell, however, spent so much of his life in Germany that his music is more German than American.

Not until the twenties of the present century did American composers begin to come into their own. By this time the character of the audiences had changed. A number of men and women who had sponsored orchestras and opera houses to obtain publicity found to their surprise that they actually liked good music. Famous musicians who went on tour had contributed to the musical education of thousands of people who lived in or near small towns. In addition, more and more immigrants had arrived from countries with musical traditions, and audiences became larger and more diversified.

Phonograph records made it possible for music, popular, concert, or operatic, to reach a still wider audience, and frequent radio broadcasts enabled the majority of Americans to listen to almost any music they desired.

If most Americans were slow to become acquainted with the best of European music, Europeans were just as slow to realize that American music had something unique to offer. Negro blues and jazz were completely different from European music in melody, rhythm, and harmony. A few native composers, suspicious of any music that was too popular with the average person, tried to avoid the use of jazz idioms in their own work. But the most gifted of twentieth-century European composers, such as Debussy, Ravel, and Stravinsky, were fascinated by it, and today there is hardly a serious composer, European or American, whose compositions do not in some way reflect the influence of jazz.

George Gershwin (1898–1937)

Born in Brooklyn, George Gershwin received all of his musical training in the United States. By the time he was sixteen, he was working as a "song plugger," a person responsible for introducing popular songs to singers and dance bands in the hope that the performers would sing and play them in public and make them popular.

It was not long before George was writing his own songs, and by the time he was twenty-five, he was a highly successful composer of popular music. But his interest in music extended beyond Tin Pan Alley, the area in New York where the popular-music publishers had their offices, and he wrote *Rhapsody in Blue* for piano and orchestra. Its melodies, rhythms, and harmonies, and his skillful use of jazz and blues in a serious concert

109. *George Gershwin, also a gifted painter, with his portrait of Arnold Schönberg. (Courtesy Ira Gershwin)*

piece made it a sensational success. He also wrote two piano concertos, as well as a sort of tone poem, *An American in Paris.* His major work, the jazz opera *Porgy and Bess,* has been performed all over the world.

While composing the score for a film in the summer of 1937, he collapsed, it was first thought, of overwork and a nervous breakdown. The diagnosis, however, was faulty, and he died several weeks later of a brain tumor.

Charles Ives (1874–1954)

While Gershwin was still a child, Charles Ives, an insurance broker, had been composing music at home, isolated from any contact with professional musicians. He spent his life in New England, and his music is based on New England folk music, hymns, and way of life. However, his compositions, with their strange, complicated harmonies, rhythms, and instrumentation, baffled many listeners. He did not receive an attentive hearing until he was past fifty, and he is now recognized as a major American talent.

Aaron Copland (1900–   )

Unlike Gershwin or Ives, Aaron Copland, also born in Brooklyn, had a thorough musical education in the United States and abroad. His music has been listened to attentively and appreciatively from the beginning. He has written many compositions, not only for concert hall, but for films and the theater as well. Two of his ballets, *Rodeo* and *Appalachian Spring,* are especially popular. He combines his technical skill with his feelings for American folk music, as well as jazz.

Leonard Bernstein (1918–   )

Leonard Bernstein, born in Massachusetts, received all of his excellent musical training in the United States. He has composed successfully for concert, musical comedy, ballet, and opera, is a prominent conductor and performer, and has performed invaluable service to music by his interesting talks on television.

There are so many distinguished American composers that it is impossible to name them all. However, Samuel Barber (1910–   ), whose works are played very frequently, not only

110. Leonard Bernstein and Aaron Copland, distinguished American composers, as conductor and soloist at a rehearsal. (Courtesy Columbia Records)

in the United States, but in Europe, and has had his operas successfully produced in leading opera houses throughout the world, must be cited, as must Italian-born Gian-Carlo Menotti (1911–   ), who reversed the usual procedure and completed his musical studies in the United States. Menotti is especially well known for his operas, for which he himself generally writes the librettos.

American conservatories are producing many fine performers and young composers, and the faculties of these musical schools include outstanding musicians of both European and American heritage. The student and the public reap the benefits of this mingling of knowledge and culture.

Musical composition is also flourishing in the Latin-American countries. Outstanding was the Brazilian Heitor Villa-Lobos (c. 1884–1959), who achieved international fame by his skillful treatment of Brazilian folk music according to the techniques developed from Bach to the composers of the nineteen-fifties. Prominent among the composers who are still alive is the Mexican Carlos Chávez (1899–   ), who has written exciting music based on Indian and early Mexican folk songs and rhythms.

The United States has now, to a large extent, replaced Europe as the center of the musical world. As one result of the devastation caused by two World Wars, composers and performers were forced to uproot themselves from their native lands and many have made their homes here, adding additional vitality to an already lively American music.

XI

MODERN COMPOSERS

The twentieth century has brought about tremendous changes in every aspect of our daily lives. Fundamental discoveries in science have been applied, not only to the creation of such spectacular products of the human imagination as supersonic planes, space ships, and computers, but to the production of such prosaic objects as deep-frozen foods, plastic containers, and electric broilers as well.

The painters, writers, and musicians of the twentieth century have been subjected to all the material changes that the century has brought. War and revolution, on a scale that no previous society has ever known, have also shaped their thoughts and given new directions to their imaginations.

Many composers, familiar with the great musical works of the past, have decided that the methods used to create these works are of little value in the present. In no music of past centuries has there been so conspicuous a lack of traditional harmony and such emphasis on dissonance. Dissonance has become a symbol of the clash of wills in our daily lives. To increase the dissonance, some composers have written into their scores the roar of an onrushing train, the hammering of rivets, or the explosions of bombs.

Arnold Schönberg (1847–1951)

An early apostle of dissonance—but without the bombs—was Arnold Schönberg. Born in Austria, he started his career as a romantic composer, and his string sextet *Verklärte Nacht (Trans-*

111. *A nineteenth-century cartoonist's view of music of the future, cats yowling.* (*New York Public Library*)

figured Night) became very popular. Schönberg soon became dissatisfied with the composition of romantic music and turned to music constructed on what was called a twelve-tone scale, as well as to "atonal" music, in which the tones belonged to no single scale. He also wrote songs in *sprechgesang*, or speech-song, the words being half spoken, half sung.

A refugee from Hitler, Schönberg died in the United States, poor and frustrated. His theories had attracted many disciples, but during his life his music had never been popular with concert audiences, who found difficulty in listening to compositions that contained neither familiar harmony nor recognizable melody. The past few years, however, have seen a revival of interest in Schönberg's work.

Paul Hindemith (1895–1963)

Paul Hindemith, born in Hanau, Germany, decided while still a child that he was going to be a professional musician. When his parents opposed him, Paul, at the age of eleven, left home and supported himself by playing the piano, clarinet, and saxophone in movie houses, restaurants, cafés, and dance halls. The money he earned playing popular tunes supported his studies of more serious music, and he became a master violist.

At thirty he was already director of the opera in Frankfort. He left to become a member of a string quartet and later was appointed professor of music in Berlin. In a few years he was recognized as one of the leaders of the "atonal" school of modern music in Germany. Hindemith felt that music should serve a purpose in life apart from the beauty of its sound, and he aimed, as did several other composers, for usefulness in music. Whether he achieved this purpose or not, his music is interesting to listen to.

When the nazis rose to power, they outlawed most modern music as "Jewish" or "bolshevik" music, and although Hindemith was neither a Jew nor a bolshevik, he left Germany. Like many other musicians, he did not want to remain in a country where his mere presence would be interpreted as indicating support of the nazi regime, while at the same time he would have to smother his creative imagination and write only music that pleased his masters. During the war years he settled in the United States, where he became chairman of the department of music at Yale University. He returned to Europe in 1953 and lived in Switzerland until his death.

Despite the frightening name of "atonality," Hindemith's music has a great deal of humor and charming melody. He was a master orchestrator and wrote in many forms. Violists in particular are grateful to him for the new compositions he added to the repertoire of his favorite string instrument.

Igor Stravinsky (1882–   )

Igor Stravinsky is a Russian composer who had originally intended to become a lawyer and changed his mind at the age of twenty. He became famous in 1913, when a Paris audience hissed

112. Igor Stravinsky conducting. (Courtesy Columbia Records)

the performance of *Le Sacre du printemps* (*The Rite of Spring*), a new ballet set to his music. The audience objected both to the music and to the story of the ballet, which was a sophisticated presentation of primitive life. Today *The Rite of Spring* is accepted as one of the most powerful works of our century.

During the next fifty-odd years, Stravinsky constantly sought new ways in which to express himself. He changed his style of composition from one work to the next, deliberately avoiding the Russian qualities of his first works, and he is now known as an *eclectic* composer, one who adapts from different sources the methods and materials that suit his own purposes.

Stravinsky left Russia before the revolution of 1917 and did not return for five decades. He spent many years in Paris before moving to the United States. His ideas and his tremendous output of music have influenced musical composition all over the world.

Stravinsky's failure to return deprived the Russians of an eminent composer. It is clear that under the conditions that prevailed in the Soviet Union he would not have been allowed to experiment as he did later on outside Russia. Nevertheless, despite the lack of complete freedom, some Soviet composers have attained international fame. Chief among them are Serge Prokofiev and Dmitri Shostakovich.

Serge Prokofiev (1891–1953)

The son of a well-to-do estate manager, Serge Prokofiev grew up in a cultured middle-class home. His mother, a fine pianist who was his first teacher, could not help recognizing his great talent, for Prokofiev composed by the age of six, and completed an opera when he was nine. His ability to learn soon outstripped his mother's ability to teach, and at twelve, Prokofiev became a student at the St. Petersburg Conservatory, where he studied orchestration with Rimsky-Korsakov.

It was as a concert pianist that he first became known to the public, and his earliest published compositions were for the piano.

113. *Serge Prokofiev.* (*Novosti Press Agency*)

But he did not restrict his compositions to that instrument, and his *Classical Symphony* was one of many works that were widely played.

During the revolutionary period, he left Russia and lived for a time in Paris, where he composed music for the ballets produced by a fellow exile, Serge Diaghilev. The next few years he traveled all over the world and was acclaimed everywhere.

In 1934, somewhat surprisingly, he returned to Russia, where he wrote music for ballets, films, theatrical presentations, and concert performance. His *Peter and the Wolf,* enjoyed by adults as well as children, was originally written for a children's theater at a time when it became evident that the nazi regime in Germany was preparing to attack Russia, and it was in a way a warning to wolves and other predatory animals. As a more direct warning Prokofiev wrote the cantata *Alexander Nevsky,* first heard as music for a film of the same name. The film, which owed much of its effect to the power of Prokofiev's music, reminded friends and enemies alike of a historic battle in which the German invaders, the Teutonic Knights, were destroyed by the Russians, led by Prince Alexander Nevsky.

Prokofiev continued to compose music for ballets, of which *Romeo and Juliet* and *Cinderella* are the best known, as well as symphonies, operas, and concertos. Although some of his work did not please Soviet authorities, and he was occasionally censured, Prokofiev regarded himself as a Soviet composer, and his world fame enabled him to shrug off the condemnation of critics who knew nothing about music. His compositions are replete with a driving energy, satiric wit, and lovely melody.

Dmitri Shostakovich (1906–   )

Born to middle-class parents in St. Petersburg, Dmitri Shostakovich, like Prokofiev and other composers, received his first music lessons from his mother, an accomplished pianist. He did not, however, decide to be a musician until he was eleven or twelve, when he enrolled in the local conservatory. This had been the St. Petersburg Conservatory; as World War I progressed, it became the Petrograd Conservatory, and later the Leningrad Conservatory.

At the Petrograd Conservatory, Shostakovich studied composition as well as piano. The period following the various revolutions was a time of hardship for people of all classes, and Dmitri, although recognized at the conservatory as an outstanding talent, had to help support his mother and sisters by playing the piano in a movie theater.

His first symphony was performed when he was only eighteen, and its success took him out of the movie theater and gave him an international reputation. Aside from several visits abroad, Shostakovich has lived in the Soviet Union all his life, and considers himself a Soviet composer, dedicated to the principles of

114. *Dmitri Shostakovich (left) at a rehearsal of one of his works in the United States. The conductor is Eugene Ormandy. (Courtesy Columbia Records)*

socialism. Several of his works have been sharply criticized by Soviet political leaders, and their criticism has influenced some of his compositions. However, in late years, he has been relatively unhampered by political interference, and even during the worst period his compositions were performed and he was able to go on with his work.

During World War II he served as an air-raid warden in Leningrad, until the government insisted on removing him to a safer place. Shostakovich has written symphonies, concertos, opera, ballets, and chamber music, and continues to lead an active and creative musical life.

115. Edgar Varèse reading the score of an electronic composition that is being played back on a tape recorder. (Courtesy Presto-Bogen from Franco Colombo, Inc.)

In the United States and Europe, in addition to the composers who have obtained recognition, there are numerous *avant-garde*, or vanguard, composers who are strenuously seeking it.

One avant-garde composer has composed fifteen minutes of silence. It is uncertain how he will collect royalties from the sale of sheet music or records. Others pluck the strings of pianos and treat other familiar instruments in unfamiliar ways.

A composer who remained in the avant-garde from the beginning of his long musical career until his death was Edgar Varèse (1885–1965). Varèse had a scientific education that influenced his ideas about musical composition. He wrote compositions with such titles as *Ionization*, and *Density 21.5*, the latter a solo for platinum flute (the density of platinum is 21.5).

Varèse was also interested in finding objects that could serve as unconventional musical instruments, and he explored the possibilities of using electronic devices to produce unusual sounds. Much of the electronic music that was composed by him and by others who followed in his footsteps is fascinating in its novelty. Unfortunately, some of the fascination disappears on rehearing, and electronic music is not often played at concerts.

One difficulty that confronts the electronic composer is the expense involved in playing his instrument. A combination of electronic devices is not only costly on its own account, but needs an electronic expert to keep it in good condition (unless the composer is one of those rare musicians who are their own experts), and

116. Electronic computer-composer at the University of Illinois. (Courtesy Dr. Lejaren Hiller)

sometimes requires so much current that it may blow the fuses of an ordinary house or apartment. Moreover, the very presence of the composer, who as a material body has an electrical capacity, can alter the tones that are produced.

In one relatively simple electronic instrument, the theremin, the performer produces sounds that differ in pitch and quality merely by waving his hands in front of the instrument. Ordinary music notation, so painfully developed during the past thousand years, is of little use for the theremin or any other electronic instrument, and composers who write for electronic instruments tend to improvise, recording their inspirations on tape at the very moment of conception, and revising later by cutting and splicing the tape.

If we accept as music any set of notes that appears on music paper, we can regard modern computers as composers. Like many of the avant-garde composers, and unlike the great composers of the past, a computer has no idea of how the music it has written will sound, and there is as yet no record of any masterpieces that have been produced by composer-computers.

Nor is there much hope that such masterpieces will be produced in the near future. A computer, having no emotions, cannot turn out music that appeals to the emotions of a human listener. It can compose only according to the rules laid down for it; this leaves no room for the inspired breaking of rules, or for any other kind of inspiration.

In general, modern audiences have shown little liking for avant-garde music, whether produced by man or machine. They tend to be bored and annoyed by it. As has been true throughout history, audiences respond to music that inspires, ennobles, and enriches their spirits.

What of the future? Will it reveal composers of the stature of Bach, Beethoven, and Mozart? One thing that is certain is that the Bachs and Beethovens of the future will compose quite differently from the Bachs and Beethovens of the past. And it may be many years before composers in a new style are recognized for the masters they are. Bach's fame was clouded for more than half a century before he began to win his rightful place among the

117. Still Music by Ben Shahn. A possibly prophetic painting of the concert stage of the future as computer-performers become the best interpreters of computer-composers. (Courtesy Phillips Collection, Washington)

immortals. Beethoven, on the other hand, was appreciated at his true worth almost from the beginning of his career, but his musical reputation too has had its ups and downs.

Of the composers now at work, which will be considered great masters a hundred years from now? We have no idea. We—and the audiences of the future—can only wait and listen.

XII

HALF THE HUMAN RACE

The reader may have noted what appears to be a rather strange omission: of the many great and near-great composers we have listed, only one has been a woman. Women have been outstanding performers, and one of the most famous teachers of contemporary composers is a Frenchwoman, Nadia Boulanger (1887–   ). She and her sister, Lili (1893–1918), were the first two women to win the *Prix de Rome*, a prize given solely for talent in composition. Nevertheless, their own music is rarely if ever played.

Many women have composed music (the name of Clara Schumann comes to mind), but what has prevented them from composing music of such beauty that their works would be part of the concert repertoire?

Was it the Catholic Church, because it did not permit them to become church musicians? There are other churches, and none of the evidence indicates that non-Catholic women have written better music than Catholic women. Was it discrimination by male musicians? There has been discrimination against women performing, but our leading symphony orchestras include women instrumentalists as well as men. Was it lack of dedication? Perhaps. But many women have shown fierce dedication to their careers in acting, singing, and writing. Why not in composing?

None of these reasons, in itself, appears to be valid. Perhaps it is a combination of all three that has prevented women from composing great music. We cannot be sure. We have said that music is many languages. Now we must add that while the female half of the human race is able to understand the languages of music spoken by others, and can express the musical thoughts of others, it has so far not uttered worth-while thoughts of its own.

We can only hope that in this respect, at least, the future of music will be different from the past.

APPENDIX

One Hundred Compositions for Your Basic Music Library
Selected by Martin Bookspan, Program Director of Radio Station
WQXR, New York City

Bach, Johann Sebastian
    Brandenburg Concertos
    Mass in B Minor
    The Passion According to Saint
      Matthew
Bartók, Béla
    Concerto for Orchestra
Beethoven, Ludwig van
    Piano Concerto #4 in G
    Piano Concerto #5 in E Flat,
      "Emperor"
    Violin Concerto in D
    Missa Solemnis in D
    Symphony #3 in E Flat
    Symphony #5 in C Minor
    Symphony #6 in F, "Pastoral"
    Symphony #7 in A
    Symphony #9 in D Minor
    "Moonlight" and "Pathétique"
      Piano Sonatas (The Sonatas
      Nos. 14 in C Sharp Minor and
      8 in C Minor)
    String Quartet No. 14 in C Sharp
      Minor
    Trio No. 7 in B Flat, "Archduke"
    Violin & Piano Sonata #9 in A,
      "Kreutzer"

Berlioz, Hector
    Romeo and Juliet
    Symphonie Fantastique
Bizet, Georges
    Carmen
Brahms, Johannes
    Piano Concerto #1 in D Minor
    Piano Concerto #2 in B Flat
    Violin Concerto in D
    Double Concerto in A Minor
    Piano Quartet #1 in G Minor
    Symphony #1 in C Minor
    Symphony #4 in E Minor
    A German Requiem
Britten, Benjamin
    War Requiem
Bruckner, Anton
    Symphony #9 in D Minor
Chopin, Frédéric
    Piano Sonatas Nos. 2 in B Flat
      Minor and 3 in B Minor
    Fourteen Waltzes
Copland, Aaron
    Appalachian Spring
Debussy, Claude
    La Mer
    Preludes for Piano

Dvořák, Antonin
  Cello Concerto in B Minor
  Symphony #8 in G°
  Symphony #9 in E Minor, "From
    the New World"°°
  ° sometimes erroneously listed as
    #4
  °° sometimes erroneously listed
    as #5
Franck, César
  Symphony in D Minor
Gershwin, George
  Rhapsody in Blue
  An American in Paris
Grieg, Edvard
  Piano Concerto in A Minor
Handel, George Frederic
  Messiah
  The Water Music
Haydn, Franz Joseph
  Symphony #94 in G, "Surprise"
  Missa Solemnis in D Minor,
    "Lord Nelson Mass"
Liszt, Franz
  Piano Concertos Nos. 1 in E Flat
    and 2 in A
  Piano Music
Mahler, Gustav
  Das Lied von der Erde
  Symphony #1 in D, "Titan"
Mendelssohn, Felix
  Symphony #3 in A Minor, "Scot-
    tish"
  Symphony #4 in A, "Italian"
  Violin Concerto in E Minor
  A Midsummer Night's Dream
Mozart, Wolfgang Amadeus
  Clarinet Quintet in A
  Don Giovanni
  The Marriage of Figaro
  Piano Concerto #20 in D Minor
  Symphony #40 in G Minor
  Symphony #41 in C, "Jupiter"
Mussorgsky, Modest
  Boris Godunov
  Pictures at an Exhibition

Paganini, Niccolò
  Violin Concerto #1 in D
Prokofiev, Serge
  Peter and the Wolf
  Symphony #5 in B Flat
Puccini, Giacomo
  La Bohème
  Madama Butterfly
  Tosca
Rachmaninoff, Sergei
  Piano Concerto #2 in C Minor
Ravel, Maurice
  Daphnis and Chloé
  L'Enfant et les Sortilèges
Rimsky-Korsakov, Nicholas
  Scheherazade
Saint-Saëns, Camille
  Symphony #3 in C Minor, "Or-
    gan"
Schubert, Franz
  Quintet in A for Piano & Strings,
    "Trout"
  Quintet in C for Strings
  Symphony #8 in B Minor, "Un-
    finished"
  Symphony #9 in C, "Great"
Schumann, Robert
  Piano Concerto in A Minor
  Piano Quintet in E Flat
  Symphony #4 in D Minor
Shostakovich, Dmitri
  Symphony #5
Sibelius, Jean
  Symphony #2 in D
  Symphony #5 in E Flat
Strauss, Richard
  Don Juan
  Till Eulenspiegel's Merry Pranks
  Don Quixote
  Der Rosenkavalier
Stravinsky, Igor
  Petrouchka
  Le Sacre du printemps
Tchaikovsky, Peter Ilyitch
  Piano Concerto #1 in B Flat
    Minor

INDEX

ABOUT THE AUTHORS

DOROTHY AND JOSEPH SAMACHSON, as a team, have written books about the theater and the opera; they have written about gold digging and the city of Rome. She is also the author of a book about ballet and he has published a book about the human skeletal system.

Mrs. Samachson is the musician of the family, having played piano in all kinds of places from the Metropolitan Opera in New York City to a supper club atop a Chicago hotel. Dr. Samachson, on the other hand, is a research organic chemist, who is now working with the Metabolic Research Unit of the Veterans Administration Hospital in Hines, Illinois.

Both of them are Easterners, Mrs. Samachson being from New York and Dr. Samachson coming from New Jersey. They now make their home in Oak Park, Illinois, where they live with their son, Michael, and their black cocker spaniel. Their daughter, Miriam, is the wife of a scientist who is presently doing research in Scandinavia.

Date Due